EDUCATION, NIHILISM AND SURVIVAL

EDUCATION, NIHILISM AND SURVIVAL

DAVID HOLBROOK

Darton, Longman & Todd

First published in 1977 by
Darton, Longman & Todd Ltd,
89 Lillie Road, London SW6 1UD

© David Holbrook, 1977

ISBN 0 232 51384 8

The author is grateful for help with this work, to the Elmgrant Trust
(as 'writer-in-residence' at Dartington, 1971–3); to Downing
College, Cambridge (as 'Assistant Director of English Studies',
1973–5); and to the Arts Council for a grant in 1976.

Printed in Great Britain by the Anchor Press Ltd
and bound by William Brendon & Son Ltd,
both of Tiptree, Essex

CONTENTS

Gradually, at first unnoticed but growing more and more pressing, possibilities for a complete reorientation of view will make themselves felt, pointing to new dimensions. Questions never before asked will arise; fields of endeavour never before entered, correlations never before grasped or radically understood, will show themselves. In the end they will require that the total sense of philosophy, accepted as 'obvious' throughout all its historical forms, be basically and essentially transformed ... In this regard, the tragic failure of modern psychology in particular, its contradictory historical existence, will be clarified and made understandable: that is, the fact that it had to claim (through its historically accumulated meaning) to be the basic philosophical science, while this produced the obviously paradoxical consequences of the so-called 'p-sychologism'.

I seek not to instruct but only to lead, to point out and describe what I see. I claim no other right than that of speaking according to my best lights, principally before myself but in the same manner also before others, as one who has lived in all its seriousness the fate of a philosophical existence.

Edmund Husserl, *The Crisis of European Sciences and Transcendental Phenomenology*, p. 18.

Chapter One

MISCHIEF AT WORK AND THE TREACHEROUS INTELLECTUAL

The introductory quotation from Husserl should indicate that I am concerned with a problem of psychology and philosophy.

Our unprofitable intellectual atmosphere in England is preserved by absurd denials of certain areas of radical thought. English philosophy has been bankrupt for years, attached to a triumphant logical positivism and an analytical technique that greets every real problem with the disdainful cry, 'Ah! Non-philosophy!' In psychology, under Eysenck's influence, every investigation of the inner life is dismissed as 'amateur psychology'. It is even claimed that there is no such thing as 'philosophical anthropology'. On what grounds? There is, indeed, such a discipline, which belongs, in Husserl's perspective, to a respectable and well-established continental philosophical tradition. Yet such areas of thought are often greeted by British intellectuals with hostility and dismissal.

How then can we enter the subject of nihilism in our current culture? The writings of Viktor Frankl, who held Freud's old chair at Vienna, will often be referred to in this book. Frankl survived Auschwitz, and wrote about this experience philosophically. *He saw that the death camps were constructed at the desks of German nihilistic philosophers.* He sees in our attitudes to life, and in the way in which our young are educated, a 'living nihilism', and a 'tendency to devaluate and depreciate that which is human in man'.One of his most important contributions was to the seminar of scientists, the Alpbach Seminar, organised by Arthur Koestler and Robert Smithies, with such scientists as C. H. Waddington and W. H. Thorpe, published as *Against Reductionism*. I begin from there.

1

My approach is phenomenological: that is, it pays attention to the meanings of consciousness. *What happens to consciousness is the most important thing in the world.* And my argument is all around the question of how we approach human problems, of meaning and morality: my case is that our approaches today to the study of man have yielded little, and are essentially dead, because they cling to positivism – that is, to an approach which demands that nothing must be regarded as real which cannot be found by empirical science and rational methods, by 'objectivity'. Since the whole problem with which I want to deal belongs to 'psychic reality', to man's 'inner world', to his moral being, and to the subjective life, there can be no debate unless we are prepared to recognise the bankruptcy of positivism, and the failure of 'objectivity' to give an adequate account of existence, and are prepared to find new modes of enquiry.

Frankl stands firmly for such a recognition, and his work is taken seriously by distinguished scientists and psychologists. Frankl made a plea for 'the human dimension'. The trouble today, he suggested, was not that scientists were specialising, but that specialists are generalising. The scientific *généralisateur terrible* turned biology into biologism and psychology into psychologism. Everything thus tended to be explained in 'nothing but' terms. It was necessary to restore the human dimension, and to recognise that if human phenomena are turned into mere epiphenomena, by suggesting that 'values and meanings are nothing but defence mechanisms and reaction formations', this reductionism is a mask for nihilism. No-one, he declared, is prepared to die for their 'reaction formations' and even less for their 'defence mechanisms': they *are* willing to die for their *meanings*.

> The true nihilism of today is reductionism. Although Jean-Paul Sartre has put the word *néant* into the title of his main philosophical work, the true message of existentialism is not nothingness, but the *no-thingness* of man – that is to say a human being is no thing, a person is not one thing among other things.
>
> *Against Reductionism*, p. 398

Frankl is concerned to resist that implicit reduction of man to an object, or to a mechanical organism, which is taught in many areas of education. He records his own protest as a youth to one of his scientific teachers: 'Dr. Fritz, if this is true, what meaning, then, does life have?' He declares that our children and students are taught, by a reductionist science, that life is meaningless, and the result, he suggests, is the 'existential vacuum' found in many lives. How, in the face of this existential frustration, do we uphold self-actualisation, by 'living out the self-transcendent quality of human existence'?

We are subjected continually, not least in the Arts, and in the Humanities in Education, to a new dogma, to a metaphysic, whose assumptions are nihilistic – there is nothing to believe in, all former values are discredited, life can have no meaning. Man's life has no moral dimension, and his strivings are absurd.

While a great deal in this new attitude is concerned with 'freedom', and 'truth', it is in fact devoted to an unrecognised set of beliefs which must not be questioned. For the view that man's life must be absurd is only tenable so long as the universe remains that delineated by Newton and Gallieo, so long as the prevalent view is mechanistic, seeing all as 'matter in motion', operating only by chance and necessity. If these views of reality were true, there could be no response except one of futility and despair: but may it not be that these views of the world are false? Michael Polanyi, in *Meaning,* concludes that 'modern science cannot properly be understood to tell us that the world is meaningless and pointless, that it is absurd' (p. 181). The modern myth that it is so is based on profound misunderstandings of science and philosophy. Yet this nihilism, implicit in so much science, is reinforced by our culture both inside and outside college. My son, taking his 'A' levels, is studying *Waiting for Godot*: in his notes, supplied by his Humanities teacher, he is told that although Beckett tells us that there is no point in existence, and that no attempt to find life meaningful will succeed, this is 'life-affirming'. If I open my *Times,* I find a review of a play by Durrenmatt. The gods are indifferent, and men are 'pitiful victims of one another'. A planet is to explode. On Earth, people behave with exasperating folly. Troops die for no reason. Hippies

3

have babies for no reason either. Prisoners move from torture to firing squad, lovers die helplessly, when their oxygen expires. It is, apparently, all very witty and intellectual. Yet it is sheer nihilism, rapturously enjoyed, and under the surface accepted as if it had a 'scientific' basis.

I go down to my local village Memorial Hall, to a jumble sale. There I buy a book published by Lorrimer Publications, called *Savage Cinema*. The pictures in this are violent, sadistic, perverted and pornographic. The roll of names of village men, killed in two World Wars, makes me reflect on the historical meaning of this document, and its phenomenological significance. What would they think of it, as a manifestation of the 'freedom' for which they fought? In my mind is the symbol of the 'death camp' in the work of Sylvia Plath. She was fascinated by these camps, and identified with their inmates. But, I believe, she did so not so much out of compassion and horror, but because she had become addicted to the negative side of her personality, her malignant animus. Her 'death camps' stood for the delicious feeling she had developed, in giving herself up to the joys of evil, because of the dreadful logic of her death-circuit. In desperation of ever finding meaning in her existence, she gave herself up to the joys of hatred, to obtain what satisfaction she could out of that. Thinking of the death camps reinforced her mental rage. She felt a deep satisfaction in ultimate brutality and death, without being able to explain it, or discriminate against it.

In one of the illustrations in *Savage Cinema* a naked girl was shown, being humiliated in a bath house. The picture had a salacious caption, and it was obvious, phenomenologically speaking, that this event was presented for the amusement of the audience, and the reader. That is, the viewers were invited to gloat on the debasement of the woman, and to feel a perverted satisfaction. They were invited to enjoy the 'depreciation of everything that is human in man'. They were thereby seduced into the philosophical depreciation to which Frankl refers, and so into the very impulse which created the concentration camps.

When I return home, perhaps I take up my *Times* newspaper again. On the Arts Page (27th April 1976) I read

4

two reviews. One is of a show called *Cycle Sluts*, headed 'Perverse Delight'. Some American actors in black leather bikinis strip off to reveal 'oil-funnelled breasts and tight g-strings which rather fail to hide their distinctive male parts.' Flaunting ambi-sexuality, they sing of flagellation and transvestism. A masochistic song, called 'Nasty', goes 'Baby, I'm born to be bruised'. They give a demented, drug-informed, reading of *Little Women*, while *You Made Me Love You* is sung to the thumping of chains, with an 'inventive' leg-flashing display, *Feel My Thigh*. Mr. Irving Wardle, alongside, reviews with enthusiasm a drag show from France, in which 'Jesus Joy of Man's Desiring' is 'geared up' to accompany a '*Clockwork Orange* number': the Mozart Requiem serves as a parody of *Jesus Christ Superstar* with Herod in black stockings. One has to pinch oneself to realise one is reading the *Times:* the most shocking thing is the cool, approving, tone of reviewers, who should know better when confronted with nihilism.

What is noticeable in such shows, and the reviews which approve them, is the malicious and militant assault on human values. Every positive is turned into a chaotic black joke, hate and perversion. Yet one of the most significant aspects of the whole development is the absence of protest, and the way in which debate is suppressed, even as the incidents in the cultural realm grow close to the psychotic. For example, one of the things which has concerned me as an educationist is the exploitation of children. In an article in *The Observer* ('The Basis of Perversion', 9 April, 1972), Dr. Mary Miles made it clear that, in her experience as a child psychotherapist, children were suffering by being exposed to cultural debasement. She feared that some adults used their talents to seduce children. This made it more difficult for them to grow up sexually, and it also made it difficult for them to control their aggression. This view was confirmed in private communications I have had with Dr. Leslie Bartlett, the psychiatrist investigating the rising incidence in his area, around Southampton, of adolescent suicide attempts, after the Tina Wilson case. He told me that he thought exposure to too-adult forms of sexuality, and anxieties about 'boy-friends' such as

5

are inculcated by the 'pop' world, had a good deal to do with the inability of some young girls to tolerate life.

There is also an element in the present trend, whereby adults (unconsciously) seem to *want* to harm children. Phenomenologically speaking, this is also part of the nihilism. Nihilism belongs to a desperate failure of meaning, and this in turn is a forfeiture of the future. As with brain-damaged patients, we have lost confidence in the future, and cling in panic to the immediate sensation. The child, however, is the future, and symbolises those protensions towards the future which we hold within us. Moreover, the child also symbolises the 'unborn', and otherwise vulnerable, elements within us, which have never grown up. He represents what W. R. D. Fairbairn has called 'the regressed libidinal ego' – that is, the hungry child-self in each of us which yearns to be satisfied. The satisfaction desired was once the body-satisfactions of the breast. But it contained then, in our infancy, a psychic element. It was a hunger to be *confirmed,* and thus given a sense of meaning. Traditionally, as in the image of the virgin and child, the infant is the symbol of emerging meaning, of love and confirmation. But it is also our hidden and feared weakness and reminds us of the pains of responsibility.

Thus today, the child is a symbol of those weaknesses which belong to being human, and are hated. In a film called *El Tropo* a little naked boy of seven was seen, clutching a teddy-bear, as he is exposed to violent scenes of rape, mutilation and murder. In *The Nightcomers* some children were shown watching sadistic sexual acts and imitating them. In *Le Souffle au Coeur* a boy of fifteen was shown seducing his mother. A programme of a local Film Festival described a film in which a young girl's genital was shown 'seething with maggots'. Reports from America speak of poor parents selling their children to the pornographers: Americans spend over £500m a year on pornography involving children.

Before our culture became corrupt we would shudder at such sinister attacks on the child, perversions of the normal impulse to love and defend him. Yet almost every intellectual with whom one raises such questions today will defend or deny them, and adopt what can only be described as a very

6

special air of detached amorality. Only by very painful processes can we begin to recover from such decadence. The most striking example of this unreal detachment is perhaps that of Charles Newman in *The Art of Sylvia Plath,* where he recognises that there are schizoid elements in her work, and admits that there may be objections to her suicide: but none of this must be raised, in our response to her poetry. Our aesthetic enjoyment of art must be undisturbed by any consideration of its schizoid moral inversion, or its nihilism. Raymond Durgnat has argued in *Books and Bookmen,* that we must measure our degree of enjoyment of a film like *A Clockwork Orange* against the number of victims of gangs of youths who burn alive or murder in imitation of the film. How many may be maimed or killed, so that we may enjoy a satisfying experience? Whatever may suffer, it must not be our 'right' to indulgence in perverted fantasy and moral inversion.

So, we are faced with such a confusion of values that the whole question of a nihilistic culture 'grows beyond access of debate.' Without resistance, we slide into an almost paralysed acceptance of atrocities to consciousness.

This has infected education. Outside the school the child and the youth are exposed to a continual stream of films and television programmes whose message is plainly nihilistic. In school, he will have to study works which imply that human existence is meaningless, and there is no way it may be lived with purpose and authenticity. Yet the question must surely arise, where is all this nihilism taking us? Is there perhaps a path developing towards something more terrible than the death camps? Can we sustain any of those meanings and values upon which civilisation is based? Can we avoid chaos, if we do not retreat from the seductiveness of moral systems based on hate?

Here I hope to examine the problem at a deeper level of philosophy and psychology. Those who argue in favour of more brutality and nihilism in culture and education often tell us that 'we must understand the vile side of our nature', and thus to place any limitation on the imagination is a serious limitation of our 'freedom'. The significant factor, however, is that, the more 'freedom' we are given, the blacker culture becomes. One reason, evidently, is that it is <u>easier to peddle hate and perversion</u> than love and truth. There may be a sense in which people like Mr. John Calder genuinely believe that 'truth' lies in wickedness and perversion: but 'liberation' has <u>not yet meant that man's aspirations, and his new potentialities, have come to be explored</u>. What is explored, in the new world of our 'permissive' culture is the darkness, the bestiality, and the perverse. Teachers who foolishly transmit this negative 'freedom' to the classroom are doing serious harm. They have depressed children, and are placing serious limits on their capacities to find meaning in their world.

In *The Daily Telegraph* of 11 July 1974 there appeared a news item, reporting the criticisms made by a primary school teacher of a new anthology issued by Penguin Books. The reporter, David Fletcher, said that 'children are being conditioned to accept violence as an everyday occurrence by a collection of stories of death and horror in use in thousands of classrooms'.

Mr. Clive Fairweather, a teacher, said that the stories used in English classes represented a 'corruption of values'. The Penguin anthology is called *Story: an anthology of stories and pictures,* and Mr. Fairweather complained that the stories leave 'an over-riding sense of pain, violence and fear': they are about the ignorant, the trapped and the deprived. 'There are graphic descriptions of racial violence, the Ku-Klux-Klan, urban guerillas, nuclear devastation, corpses and grave-digging. There is football violence, and hooliganism, classroom violence, accidents and mutilations; in three separate stories characters lose their finger ends; Negroes, Germans and Indians, portrayed as bewildered savages, are hounded and shot with tremendous gusto.' The stories include accounts of the slaughter of rats, bears, locusts, a maimed horse, plovers, whales, sharks, bucks, porcupines, badgers, rabbits and chickens. The chicken-killing reads: 'Catching it by the leg she raised it suddenly above her head, and brought down the bleeding body on the boy's back, in blow after blow, spattering the blood all over his face and his hands.' Mr. Fairweather said 'Torturing a rabbit to death takes four pages; a man who kills rats by biting through their necks merits eleven pages; the details of badger baiting cannot be contained in less than fifteen.'

No doubt, the intention of those who compiled and published the anthology was to teach children about violence as an aspect of experience. But violence is not just a human fact: it belongs to the subjective realm, and it is bound up with meaning. We cannot ever respond to violence, especially as it is visually depicted, without an involvement, which is easily excited. What is aroused are those infantile fantasies which belong to the earliest moments of 'finding the other', of wanting to eat out the inside of the other, and fearing for the consequences. Anyone who was sensitively aware of the subjective problems of unconscious fantasy in human beings, would think twice about exposing children to such unrelieved violence without providing ample resources to 'place' it.

Violence, as Rollo May argues in *Power and Innocence*, is a compensation for a deficiency of existential security, for the loss of meaning. It is on the whole a false solution, to problems of vulnerability, and a dread of anomie or apathy. Where people are threatened with a lack of a sense of meaning, of something to set against the *Dasein* problem, the problem of deciding what meaning their lives may have before they die, they may take the path of hate and destructiveness, in desperation. This is the conclusion one comes to, after studying the 'schizoid diagnosis', made by such therapists as Fairbairn, and I have applied these phenomenological insights to the work of certain artists, whose problems were schizoid, in the sense that they could not go on living, unless they applied themselves to the problem of existence, in the face of deep psychic insecurities. If I am right in my analyses of the work of Sylvia Plath and Gustav Mahler, there are serious dangers, at the point of which the soul must choose between true and false solutions to the problem of existence. True solutions are painful – as we may hear in the most harrowing music of Mahler's *Ninth*. If an individual feels that he cannot face this pain, or that it would be hopeless to try, he may 'give himself up to the joys of hating, and get what satisfaction he can out of that'. Mahler knew this temptation, and we may hear it in the mad abandonment of the third movement of the *Ninth*. However, he

9

never gave in. But Sylvia Plath does, and at times 'cultivates her psychoses': in *Lady Lazarus, Daddy,* and *Edge,* she tries to seduce us into reckless abandonment, to the false strength of nihilism, and the death circuit which, in the end, killed her.

Discussing the above anthology of violence, Mr. Fairweather says, 'One is left with the impression that killing resolves conflicts, and confers a kind of ritual confrontation with the irrational and obscene.' This is also the message of many fashionable modern films and novels, as well as of many serious works at the heart of minority culture. In the light of 'philosophical anthropology' the message of such works must be rejected. But the pupil studying nihilistic works for 'A' level may lack all resources for dissociating himself from their message. His biology and science may well endorse the philosophical position based on natural scientism and positivism, which continue to present a world in which the only response is despair and futility. It may seem that the only 'freedom' left is that of hate.

In the work of the Polish sociologist Kiryl Sosnowski, *The Tragedy of Children Under Nazi Rule,* we may follow the deliberate corruption of morality among German children, for political purposes. This runs parallel to the similar destruction of values among our young, by the no less sinister processes of commercial conditioning. In *Culture Against Man,* Professor Jules Henry says that the arrogance of the advertiser is 'terrifyingly reminiscent of another appeal to children over the heads of their parents', meaning those of Nazism. So, we are experiencing again, 'The silent dictatorship exercised by the child over his parents within the family home', which Sosnowski delineates in pre-War Germany. In a book called *The Assault on the Child,* Ron Goulart gives an account of how advertisers seek to make children scream and writhe on the floor, in order to extract things from their parents which have been advertised by appeals to their innocence. 'You can't get that kind of reaction out of an adult'. They declare their victory with the same triumphant tone once heard in Germany:

When an adversary says – I won't come over to your camp, I am not being taken in – I reply calmly, Your child is ours already . . . your off-

10

spring have already joined the new camp . . . before long they will know nothing but the new community . . .

(Adolf Hitler, quoted in Sosnowkski).

Journalists, television producers, film producers, 'pop' manipulators, and others in Britain have generated a 'new camp' whose values and attitudes have totally broken away from the traditional values of family, church, school, university and community. Far from being a new development of the kind yearned for by Husserl, the attitude of this new 'camp' betrays it as essentially nihilistic: it recognises no focus of values to which to give account: it finds no meaning in life except hedonism and assertiveness. Yet the intellectual minority have nothing else to offer and are essentially treacherous. Even in education and the Humanities many feel there are no grounds, no values, by which to resist, and as I shall try to show, some of our own leading philosophers, like Sartre, provided a well-argued ground for this decline. In the end, it all leads, as I shall try to show, to an egoistical nihilism that would make social life and politics impossible.

It is not a question only of a change in what is *permitted* – but a deep corruption of the values by which we judge symbols and meanings in culture: it all adds up to the collapse of our meaning-system. Today we find moral chaos at the most serious level. For instance, on 4th January 1974 *The Times Literary Supplement* reviewed *le Corps Lesbien*, by Monique Wittig, published in Paris. The reviewer said:

The inamorata is told on the first page to say adieu to tenderness and affection and 'gracious abandon'. She is in for knives, machine-guns, pincers, the whip, she is going to have her skin peeled off, and the stink of her lover's intestines is going to surround them with every move they make . . . Plenty of sexual practices are referred to in the text too, but strangely enough there is nowhere the slightest trace of eroticism (or obscenity for that matter).

It is, indeed, very strange, that such obscenities are not obscene: what can 'obscene' mean? Journalists began writing in this dissociated way, when reviewing obscene shows, in order to prevent precipitating a prosecution. Gradually, it seems, they have come to believe their own lies. It is quite

11

clear that there must be in the book under review, both eroticisms of a perverted kind, and obscenity: to deny this is to do serious damage to the language and to concepts.*

By such forms of destruction of debate, the proponents of cultural debasement have created a situation in which escape seems impossible. Lewis Mumford declares quite roundly:

> From the normally creative minds of poets and artists has come an explosion of anti-life in images that correspond to the outbursts of delinquency and criminality that haunt our daily affairs and that collectively, actually threaten the existence of mankind.
>
> By a total inversion of human values, the favoured leaders and mentors of our age prefer disease to health, pornography to potent sexual experience, debasement to development.
>
> *Interpretations and Forecasts.*

The 'revolution' which has chosen these destructive paths, not least in certain areas of education, seems to believe that its position rests upon 'the best that is thought and known in the world.' The truth is, however, that certain 'philosophies' or 'models' of man which they take for gospel, like Desmond Morris's false extrapolations from science to a general philosophy of life in *The Naked Ape*, are highly questionable. In certain subjective disciplines, from philosophical biology to psychoanalytical psychology, hard-won insights completely reject the 'realism' upon which the dogmas of nihilism are based. It is, for example, highly questionable to believe that man's primary nature is based upon his 'instincts' of sex and aggression. As Abraham Maslow has said, there is a new psychology which completely alters the perspectives:

> ...: it is ... a clear confrontation of one basic set of values by another newer system of values which claims to be not only more efficient but also more true. It draws some of the truly revolutionary consequences of the discovery that human nature has been sold short, that man has a higher nature which is just as 'instinctoid' as his lower nature, and that this higher nature includes the needs for meaningful work, for responsibility, for creativeness, for being fair and just, for doing what is worthwhile and preferring to do it well.
>
> *Towards a Psychology of Being*, p.222

* Important here is a new study, *Perversion: The Erotic Form of Hatred,* Robert Stoller, Harvester Press, 1976. The denial that something is obscene is often a denial that it is full of hate.

Maslow points out that there is, in our predominant functionalistic psychology, a derogation of the desire for higher satisfactions, and an under-valuing of inward experience, with a consequent debasement of impulse. This is accompanied by a loss of creative sense of time. 'Growth and becoming and possibility necessarily point towards the future; so do the concepts of potentiality and hoping, of wishing and imagining'. Because we have lost sight of these in our philosophy and psychology, and in our culture, we are being overtaken by a loss of belief in the future – exacerbated by our attachment to instant sensation, and the 'reduction to the concrete'. Because of this, even our survival is menaced, because our morale, and our creative impulses are threatened, by a nihilism which recognises no possibility of a realisable future.

Even in 'liberal' studies, which were supposed to uphold human values, one finds the impulse to reject them. Mr. Colin Falck, for instance, writing in the *Times Literary Supplement*, (25th July 1968) said 'the point of liberal studies . . . is ultimately political: its aim is to rock the boat. Most students are young, after all, and will swim well enough if they have to.' His article is characteristic of developments in the last decade, in fashionable approaches to the Humanities, and I shall use it as a central foil to my argument:

'Modern literature has in any case set its own limits to the educational purposes to which it can be put. The concept of the 'whole man' is a useful one, but in the face of a mutilated society it may be necessary for men themselves to be divided. Matthew Arnold knew this – he is perhaps the first striking example of a man divided into earnest educator and despairing poet – and a lot of water has passed under the bridge since then. Arnold wanted literature to civilise us, but today we are coming more and more to recognise (or to remember) that the natural tendency of literature is to subvert, and that most modern literature is actually nihilistic and destructive with regard to the established order of technological society . . .'

But what about those who don't 'swim well enough'? What are the politics of their predicament? A young woman with a first in Education at Newnham writes:

I was particularly interested in your phrase 'egoistical nihilism' as this indicates clearly the state in which a majority of pupils are evidently experiencing in this school, and this state of mind is often, as you suggest, accompanied by uncontrolled aggression and violence. This, in conjunction with an inefficient educational system which offers the pupils no guidance in value-forming or rule-following behaviour is rapidly creating a society of young people who appear to lack any form of altruistic motives and principles or notions of co-operation. Consequently classes become almost impossible to control, the school environment becomes one of licence and near-chaos, with frequent exhibitions of violence which meets with little or no punishment.

Suppose we offer the pupil or student the poetry of Sylvia Plath. After a lecture I gave in Australia a student laid a poem on the bench, and went out. It read:

For Sylvia Plath (after reading 'Ariel')

father-hater
life-denyer
self-loather
you proved your point
existence isn't worth the effort
no matter how disciplined you are or how many times you die

. . .

my grief is wearisome
your blackness and silence crushes me.
Why don't you speak
am I to be your altar lamb
snuffed out before my poetry lives
you gave yourself the chance so why not me.

Marrow eater, I am my own destroyer

I will not do.

O.K. Plath you bitch, you've won, I'm through.

A group of psychotherapists later confirmed that I should have been worried. They knew what a harmful effect the fashionable pose – that you haven't lived until you've attempted suicide – has on their patients. And they confirmed that to expose a young person in a black mood to Sylvia Plath might well do them harm. It is possible for a student to go through his or her courses and to be offered few resources to draw on, to resist such nihilism.*

14

In this book I hope to work through some of these problems, and, in the end, recover the truth, which is that scientific and reasonable investigations are vindicating the existence of meaning and values rooted in love and human altruism. Again, Husserl is one important corrective: as intellectuals, we must be custodians of humanness. In the philosophy of Husserl and other phenomenologists like Binswanger there are, quite clearly, responsibilities emerging which oblige us to take on certain burdens with our knowledge. So, too, are there emerging principles in the psychology of Sullivan, Rollo May, Winnicott and Lomas, to name only a few, which suggest that human perception and effectiveness in living, for example, are bound up with the quality of our relationships, while these, in turn, are the focus of choice and action. In Marjorie Grene's work we have a serious emphasis on human responsibilities in learning: as, for instance, to the question of the way in which we treat certain classes of people as inferior beings. In existentialist thought, we have an emphasis on man making himself by his choices and actions, even in the 'old' existentialism which sees such choices as never solving the *Dasein* problem. In the 'new' existentialism, as we shall see, proper choices are bound up with 'loving communion' and our capacity to care for others. All these areas of thought are full of 'ethical principles' quite apart from those of traditional morality and religion. And I shall end by turning back to an important symposium by Maslow.

Colin Falck went on in his characteristic article to advocate that we should immerse our students in nihilistic literature, because art is fundamentally 'insurrectionary':

> the literature teacher's best motto these days is 'Mischief, thou art afoot': his hour a week is valuable not as a little bit of culture but as a little bit of disturbance. At the moment there is a tendency for liberal studies teachers to be nervous and puzzled in the face of pornography and the literature of sex and violence and to play safe by *clinging to some more wholesome view of things*, to the literature of 'commitment', or to the healthier aspects of Lawrence. Perhaps what we should be doing . . . is

---

* Ross Fitzgerald survived, and his poem is published in *The Eyes of Angels*, The Saturday Centre, Australia, 1973.

giving our students as much of the romanticism-existentialism-nihilism
traditions as they can take and helping them to come to terms with it. It
probably *will* answer to something in their own experience if only we can
admit – to them and to ourselves – that it answers to something in us.
(my italics)

Much of today's culture may actually be *corrupting* to the
sensibility, because once people are exposed to it, insofar as
they do not withdraw or reject it, they are compromised. They
become enlisted in a subtle inverted rationalization, which
gradually comes to seem logically pure and inescapable. It
must often be a grave shock to students and pupils, to find that
their educational establishment is exposing them to deeply
disturbing material, presented in a situation of trust, but
without any assistance being offered to deal with the underlying distortions of experience. They are plunged into a
darkness in which it seems impossible to believe anything.

It must surely be of urgent interest, to the sociologist and
educationist, if children and young people are being exposed
to nihilistic influences on such a scale? Yet doubtful responses
are often dismissed as 'hysterical'. In the process there may be
serious ways in which the quest for truth itself is being under-
mined. Must we abandon that quest for truth through art of
which Conrad speaks, in the Preface to *The Nigger of the Nar-
cissus*: 'art itself may be defined as a single-minded attempt to
render the highest kind of justice to the visible universe, by
bringing to light truth . . .'? If so, on what grounds?

At the time of writing the problem presents itself again in
the form of an issue of the little magazine *Ambit*, full of gross
obscenities offered in the name of poetry. At once, it becomes
impossible to speak of love in such a context, or to resist the intrusion of irony, destructiveness and cynicism. Each such experience makes it more and more impossible to uphold
humanitas, and to find the essential *telos* of philosophical enquiry. It is impossible to protect the young from this corruption, and there is little doubt that we must now speak of the
way in which exposure to such a debased culture must limit
powers of living. Already, children experience the worst
degradations, the most powerful nihilism, as in 'X' films: in
many schools it is a matter of prestige for children as young as

16

eleven to sit through these. At Dartington, when I was there, children were allowed even into uncertificated films: at Hornsea College of Art there was a course in pornography, while explicit sex education is fashionable in schools, some of it near-pornographic.

As Bertrand Russell says, if we abuse the child by bad forms of education his 'life . . . can grow less living'. Yet this truth has been seriously abandoned since the Advisory Centre for Education supported *The Little Red Schoolbook,* which told children pornography was harmless and that if they saw anything in it that 'looked interesting' they should 'try it.' '

One wonders what Mr. Falck means by his somewhat contemptuous phrase 'clinging to some wholesome view of things'? The tone is nihilistic: 'clinging' suggests retrospective, panicky old-fashionedness. Is it then for the *Humanities* teacher to reject all values which enable us to distinguish between decent and indecent, human and anti-human? In the light of the work of people like Maslow, there is no overwhelming evidence or convincing argument, in the various disciplines of what I shall call philosophical anthropology, for overthrowing the 'wholesome view of things', nor any excuse for not being able to distinguish between wholesome and unwholesome. All the implications from recent developments in psychotherapeutic psychology, philosophy and philosophical biology point the other way – towards new ethical principles which rather vindicate traditional values upholding 'wholesomeness'. They do not uphold authoritarian methods, since their whole emphasis is on autonomy. But such a reasonable belief in autonomy depends upon a parallel belief that most of us, presented with human truths, such as the 'ethical principles' emerging from psychoanalysis and existentialism, will be prepared to give assent to human values, and submit to the insights coming from distinguished minds in the Humanities. But a belief in reason can only be sustained so long as we are not overwhelmed by the irrational and by nihilism.

Interestingly, Mr. Falck links his defence of nihilism with a defence of commercialised entertainment, which finds hate, nihilism and debasement so profitable, and is endowed with

17

the power to inflict it on us. Falck accused people like myself of 'giving the impression that most of today's popular art is simply contemptible':

> contempt for today's popular culture means contempt for the very texture of the life experience of most people under the age of about thirty. Real choice between life and death are still being made in that commercialised society, and real artists are still writing about them . . .

Those who follow such a lead in throwing in their hand with commercial exploitation place their hope on what Falck calls 'contemporary non-minority products': that is, the debased products of a decadent technological society itself, and the attachment to materialistic, hedonistic living, rather than to becoming and the future.

But who is expressing contempt? It is possible that those who condemn 'pop' know how by contrast, genuine creativity in music or writing can serve the pursuit of existential freedom in every child. My impression is that the need to create often fails to find sufficient sustenance in the world outside school, while even those still at school too often fail to find creative opportunities. While recognising that certain forms of culture have become part of the texture of life of young people, our point is that these inhibit true creativity, involve them in some forfeiture of their freedom, and menace the future.*

Of course, a man may experience frustration of his natural creativity, as it seeks to fulfil the 'formative principle' in himself, by some conformist or false self. He may find himself thwarted by a dehumanizing civilisation, which offers only inadequate opportunities for the serving of goals beyond the self, or he may find himself in a cultural desert. Because of frustration or cultural starvation in many people at large, there could arise a necessary 'subversion' against conformity – what Marion Milner calls a 'creative fury' against 'compliant adap-

---

* See *The Black Rainbow* and the present author in *Discrimination and Popular Culture*, ed. Denys Thompson, Pelican. If intellectuals believe in the freedom to be exploited, the exploiters certainly do not believe in freedom of debate. When an American team of researchers examined *The Exorcist* they found it contained subliminal material to disturb the mind: Warner Brothers threatened them with the utmost rigour of the law if they published pictures from the film. See *Media Sexploitation,* Wilson Bryan Key, Prentice-Hall, 1976.

tation (see below p. 82). But the 'natural' tendency, if we are to speak of all literature, is not to 'subvert' merely, but to pursue, by constructing something upon which to rejoice, a sense of meaning. The poetry of Edward Thomas, or of Li Po, or Thomas Hardy's *Veteris Vestigia Flammae* cannot be seen as having to do with subversion in any sense, for example: nor is Roethke's, Eliot's, Lowell's or Shakespeare's poetry, nor the novels of Forster or Saul Bellow: what can Falck mean?

In teaching we experience the creative 'formative principle', in action, in the emerging human identity, in the child and adolescent – and in ourselves. We know what we mean by creativity. It is impossible to deny the fact that culture is a form of education, at whatever level. It is the embodiment of people's attitudes to themselves, and to reality. Who could disagree with this emphasis of Professor G. H. Bantock?

> Our culture, for good or ill, exercises a profound influence over us. It organises the way in which we learn to see the world in these important areas of our understanding. For instance, it provides us with a language which in itself helps to structure our attitude to the world. And the various forms of our culture provide us with a picture of ourselves, our society, and the world of nature, in ways which we assimilate as we grow up. . . When we think of different attitudes and feeling over the stretches of history we can see how important our culture is in providing us with explanations of the world we live in, and how it directs our attitudes and feelings as well as our ideas. Of course, we all add an individual and unique element to that understanding: but we are still very much at the mercy of what our culture *teaches* us about life.
>
> *Culture, Industrialization and Education* p. 2

This cultural 'teaching' is inevitably bound up with creative processes of symbolism, our natural moral sense, and our sense of meaning. It follows that it is possible for culture to teach things which are false and wrong. If culture is a primary need, what it does to consciousness is of major social importance. Yet so many are prepared to deny these truths.

Another element missing from Mr. Falck's argument, but made clear by Bantock, is that commerce and the industrialization of culture impel television and journalism to *promote* amoral attitudes, and to *seduce* the public. These people speak from what Marx called 'the icy waters of egoistical calculation', while 'the permissive society is *not* a liberated society, but one ruthlessly controlled in the interests of hedonistic consumer capitalism' (Charles Parker in *The Black Rainbow*). Aaron Esterson, the Marxist psychotherapist, has spoken to me of the 'seduction of the people' by pornography.

Of course we must recognise some of today's excesses as belonging to a determination among the rising generation to try to develop a more human way of life, in which opportunities to exert one's self-realization and *potentia* may be seized. As D. W. Winnicott wrote in *Playing and Reality*, 'It is salutary to remember that the present student unrest and its manifest expression may be in part a product of the attitude we are proud to have attached towards baby care, and child care. Let the young alter society and teach grown-ups how to see the world afresh . . .' (p. 150). The best of youth 'protest' is an assertion of 'subjectivity', even though there are many problems of preventing this revolt from taking false paths.

Even the consequences of the more humane education which we have achieved are leading to a clash between youth and a materialist society. Some young people will no longer accept that people must be brutalized to serve the 'technologico-Benthamite' myth (as F. R. Leavis calls it) of continuous expansion and material progress. These are positive radical tendencies, and the recent protests by French students (April 1976) seem perfectly justified, against a utilitarian threat to the universities as centres for the Humanities. But the strangest manifestation of recent years is that so many 'radicals' have come to be seduced into nihilistic false solutions, and into collective infections. The present writer will never forget being booed and shouted down, by the staff and students of Dartington College of Art, in 1971, for discriminating in lectures against verses of Mick Jagger, and against pornographic films shown there to children, defended by the staff and local magistrates.

Here it is sufficient to say that many individuals of weak identity, who are disturbed in their emotional life, are only too ready to fall in with an invitation to base their solutions to life's problems on the dynamics of hate. If this were not so, we would not need laws against racial discriminations, or to take

20

measures against football hooligans. The great negro leader Martin Luther King recognised the need for restraints, to reinforce people's inner morality.

> While it may be true that morality cannot be legislated, behaviour can be regulated. The law may not change the heart, but it can restrain the heartless . . . it will take education and religion to change bad internal attitudes – but legislation and court orders can control their external effects . . .

It is the disturbed youth, frustrated by a society which offers him few opportunities to find a genuine sense of self, and fails to give him a role and responsibility, who is most vulnerable to the forms of exploitation which are imposed upon him by a sexploitation commerce or fanatical immoralists. We can see an illustration of the truth of Guntrip's maxim, 'It is the weak who hate: only the strong can love.'

Imagine the appeal of the 'false solutions' abroad in our culture, to a nineteen-year-old young man who betrays his serious degree of disturbance thus:

> I am getting rather fed up with this life. When I think that this earth is just a speck in the universe it all seems so puny and futile with no reason at all. One part of the world helps people, one part invents weapons to destroy, and the other part seeks to make money out of the other two . . . I feel so frustrated at times I feel like destroying everything in sight. I sometimes envy the dead and the insane. I find walking in the early hours of the morning helps me a lot. I wish I was always in the dark, alone and quiet. I feel better then. But I get strong urges to do things . . . if I read about a big job being done or a murder I want to do the same, so that people will know I'm equal to anyone . . . I can't stand being taken as a figure of no account.
> ('B.G.' in *Young People: Problems of Adaptation to a Fragmented Society, Guild Lecture 157, Guild of Pastoral Psychology,* W. H. Allchin)

The 'pop' industry, film and television culture try to sell such young people false solutions, as a deliberate, and dishonest, commercial policy. Nik Cohn has written:

> As Manager, what Oldham did was to take everything implicit in the Stones and blow it up one hundred times . . . he turned them into everything that parents would most hate, be most frightened by. All the time he goaded them to be wilder, nastier, fouler in every way than they

21

were – they swore, sneered, snarled, and, deliberately, they came on cretinous.

It was good basic psychology*: kids might see them the first time and be not so sure about them, but then they'd hear their parents' whining about those animals, those filthy long-haired morons, and suddenly they'd be converted, they'd identify like mad.

This, of course, is bedrock pop formula; find yourself something that truly makes adults squirm and, straightaway, you have a guaranteed smash on your hands ...

Nik Cohn, A Wop Bop a Loo Bob, p. 155

After describing a scene in which thousands of girl fans had urinated out of hysterical excitement, Nik Cohn says, 'I've kept on saying how great the Stones were, all I've shown is evil and the question finally needs to be asked: what's so good about bad?' (op. cit. p. 155). Colin Falck's answer would be perhaps that such debasement is acceptable, 'because it answers to something in themselves'. But this is the danger: that we can be *corrupted, because* we have inclinations towards false solutions in ourselves. To many liberals, the human personality is largely incorruptible. If we leave matters 'open' and uncontrolled, most people will 'swim'. The imagination must be completely free, and no damage will be done. One may applaud this confidence in human rationality. But it contains a fallacious underestimation of the powers of fanatical immoralists or schizoid manipulators to enlist others in their psychopathology. The liberal rational belief is a strange one indeed in the age of Nazism, of IRA violence, of terrorist acts – such as at Lod airport, where the perpetrators declared they would go to the planet 'Orion' when they died, to start a new life.

Below I shall try to unravel some of the processes in the psyche by which such things can happen, and suggest that cultural dynamics are powerful influences. We must place a greater emphasis than the liberal rationalist on the irrational and unconscious areas of the mind. The commercial film promoter knows about these areas: they are worth money to him. The film company which made *The Exorcist*, for example,

---

* 'Psychology' here means 'corrupt exploitation of feelings'. This passage is discussed by Charles Parker in *The Black Rainbow*, as indicating a perversion of relationships between adults and adolescents.

used subliminal material, death's heads flashed on the screen, combined with noises of pigs being killed, angry bees, people in sexual acts, and people dying, to disturb the lower areas of the psyche, to promote mental sickness in those watching. I tried to raise this question in *The New Humanist*, but the Editor declared they could not publish such an article, 'because it is so far from our fundamental commitment to freedom of speech. However much we hate sadistic and irrational films etc . . . we believe that people have the right to offer them to the public . . . we are not prepared to use this hard-won freedom to attack the freedom of others.' (Private communication). This seems to imply that once the Humanists have achieved their freedom, they are not going to allow much scope for opinions with which they disagree: in this instance the audience was not to know their minds were being manipulated – how is this 'freedom'? In a footnote above I record the response of Warner Brothers: commercial exploiters and rational humanists join forces in denying the problem, while the symbolising system is abused.

The underlying problem is the recognition of the dark, unconscious area of the psyche Jung calls 'the shadow'. As Marie Louise Von Franz says, 'the shadow is exposed to collective infections to a much greater extent than is the conscious personality. When a man is alone, for instance, he feels relatively alright; but as soon as 'the others' do dark primitive things, he begins to fear that if he doesn't join in, he will be considered a fool. Thus he gives way to impulses that do not really belong to him at all'. (*Man and His Symbols*, p. 168). This is how people can be drawn into 'false solution' behaviour. The 'alien psychic factor' is the 'anima' or 'animus' in man and woman – the shadow of the other sex in one's personality, which can become malignant. There is no doubt that the connection between the individual psychology and politics is a crucial concern, where our survival is at stake. In Sylvia Plath we can see evident symbolism of a malignant animus, called 'Daddy', and, in the end, her attraction to this male element, and her repulsion of 'him', killed her.

The problem may also be seen in terms of 'true' and 'false' self, in the light of the psychotherapeutic theories of D. W.

Winnicott and Peter Lomas (see *True and False Self*). The difference is no mere semantic one. It draws attention to the latent potentialities in ourselves, which the therapist is concerned to draw out by his 'reflection' of the patient. Whatever constructs stand in the way of this development of the person may be called the 'false self' – and the problem of life is to find those dynamics which are one's genuine *potentia*. The true self is 'that which we have in ourselves to become', and it belongs to a unity of mind and body, in which the individual may feel that his choices and modes of existence are right for him – 'authentic' in the existentialist sense, and in no conflict with his essential nature. Psychotherapists speak of the 'true self' as that which the individual is 'intended to become', as shown by his dreams, which speak of unfulfilled potentialities. This raises the question – '*intended . . . by whom?*' The answer will depend on one's faith: for the aetheistic humanist, like myself, there is a recourse to words like Nisus or *Ahnung*, as used by F. R. Leavis (see *The Living Principle*).

To summarise recent psychoanalytical theories, the pattern of potential corruption which we are concerned with may be thus explained. Where the identity is weak, the individual may feel empty at the heart of his personality. He may even feel that there is an 'unborn self' lurking within him. W. R. D. Fairbairn calls this the 'Regressed Libidinal Ego' – that part of the self which is both desperately hungry to live, and which has yet 'retreated' as if to the womb. This unborn self is both feared and hated – a diagnosis born out by the imagery of, say, the poems of Sylvia Plath, where this vulnerable unborn hungry self is at the same time both an amusing little puppy ('Fido Littlesoul . . . the soul's familiar') and a terrible menace because the hunger to relate and exist threatens to eat up everyone and everything. ('I am terrified by this dark thing that sleeps in me / Looking out with its hooks for something to love'). This unborn self, and the emptiness at the heart of the identity, makes the schizoid individual feel terribly vulnerable (and, since we all experience schizoid problems, we all feel so at times). So, he or she either conforms to a 'social' identity in a nervous, automatic way; or, tries to distract the self from the problem of emptiness by bustling and compulsive activity, or

24

becomes aggressive, as a defence measure. Such False Self activity, if taken up by a group of people, seduced into assumed strength in fear of inner weakness, can become a collective infection – especially if a group of schizoid people take the ultimate flight-path from the love they fear, and 'give themselves over to the joys of hating and get what pleasure they can out of that' (see Fairbairn's *Psychoanalytical Studies of the Personality*). Examples are Hell's Angels, Ku Klux Klan, Terrorist groups, *Blousons Noirs*, and other such negative collusions. Some such groups today evidently cohere around a film (*The Wild Ones, A Clockwork Orange*) as is clear, phenomenologically, from the costumes adopted.

As Michael Polanyi has argued, the seductive and sinister appeal of such patterns of moral inversion and hate, at the philosophical level, lies in the 'logically stabler state of complete moral inversion' which nihilism seems to offer (See the essay 'Beyond Nihilism' in *Knowing and Being*).

The political dangers were discussed not long ago by the Jewish magazine *Patterns of Prejudice,** reviewing a book by two professors at Frankfurt University called *Pornotopia*. The danger is that of inadvertently fostering the barbaric potentialities in man, and so undermining important areas of meaning and value, and so, morality. Cultural immoralism 'is claiming tolerance for offences to high standards of morality, as in the case of fascist racist persecution' . . . 'The point is to ensure the evil things may be done with a clear conscience.' As in our culture today, what are promoted are 'offences to high ideals' – while the population is being told, 'You are enjoying it, aren't you? It's bestial but such fun', as were the youth in Hitler's Germany. Egoistical nihilism becomes the healthy view of the liberated: but the exploitative element, the failure of care for others is lost sight of. This Jewish magazine links the new barbarism of pornography with that of Auschwitz: over its gateway was written 'Work sets free!' – today's slogan being 'Lust sets free!'

This view of the political dangers of a recklessly exploitative culture is confirmed by Polanyi's analysis. He traces the

* Vol. 5, No. 2, April 1971.

25

development of scientific scepticism into fanatical immoralism, and quotes de Sade, who says through one of his characters, 'I have destroyed everything in my heart that might have interfered with my pleasures.' Simone de Beauvoir sees this approvingly as a 'triumph over conscience' (conscience being a bourgeois 'inhibition') and acclaims de Sade for his passionate exposure of the 'bourgeois hoax' which consists in 'erecting class-interests into universal moral principles.' Polanyi goes on:

> A great wave of anti-bourgeois immoralism sweeping through the minds of German youth in the inter-war period formed the reservoir from which the SS and SA were recruited ... they were inspired by the same truculent honesty and passion for moral sacrifice which turned the nihilists of Russia, whether romantic or scientist, into the apparatchiks of Stalinism.
>
> *Knowing and Being*, p. 17

Their morality, says Polanyi, was inverted and became immanent in brute force because a naturalistic view of man forced them into this manifestation. 'Once they are immanent, moral actives no longer speak in their own voice, and are no longer accessible to moral arguments; such is the structure of modern nihilistic fanaticism.' (p. 18).

One of the apologists for the new liberation of 'sensuality' is Susan Sontag. Writing about this apostle of a 'new culture' of the future, Martin Green said:

> Like McLuhan, Miss Sontag and Mr. Rieff believe that we are the end of the literary phase of our culture, and that along with literature will decline (as primary cultural values) literacy, privacy, individualism, the conscience, self-sacrifice, self-improvement, 'standards' culture itself in the Matthew Arnold sense. They think that the art of the future will return to its (as they believe) essential function of *releasing man's sensuality* – in the widest sense of that phrase, the whole half of our nature *which civilisation victimises*. The classic dilemma of our culture, Miss Sontag says, is the hypertrophy of the intellect at the expense of energy and sensual capability ...
>
> *A New Sensibility, Cambridge Quarterly* Winter 1966–7. (my italics)

In invoking her authorities Susan Sontag betrays her position, as does Falck, by linking 'existentialism' and nihilism. Miss Sontag simply adheres to the more nihilistic stream of European philosophy, and tries to convey the impression that this is the only 'realistic' stream of thought. But there is another stream of positive thinking about man's nature and some of her names may be claimed for it – the early Marx, for instance, and Nietzsche. Some philosophical anthropologists are fighting back against nihilism. Confident and aggressive amoral or anti-moral positions can only rest on intellectual confusion, and some falsification, not least by individuals who have a schizoid axe to grind. They may feel what they say is 'their' truth ('What I did was right for me' said one of Charles Manson's followers). But some of these people see evil as evil and also *choose* it.

Behind Susan Sontag's talk of the 'release' of 'sensuality' is an outdated philosophical position based on the quantitative natural science 'model' of man. This appeals to the anti-social elements in the intellectual world, and to those who are enabled to rationalise their own disturbed conduct, and to vindicate their own flight from life, as a 'release of instincts'. It appeals to schizoid individuals by giving validity to their immoral motives. But intellectuals ought to know better: the books are there to read.* Above all, *science* itself is taking the lead, in a rediscovery of man's potentialities and his moral being.

The lamentable truth is that the intellectual has become treacherous. Joost de Meerloo, the Dutch psychotherapist who survived Auschwitz, has said that this happens *because the intellectual does not have the courage to try to understand himself, and is a mental coward*. His betrayal of human values, health, and truth is a rejection of commitment and responsibility:

It is among the intelligentsia, and especially among those who like to play with thoughts and concepts without taking part in the cultural endeavours of their epoch, that we often find the glib compulsion to explain everything and understand nothing. Their retreat into intellectual isolation and ivory-tower philosophy is a source of such hostility and suspicion from those who receive the stones of intellectualism instead of

* E. G. *The Cult of the Fact*, Liam Hudson; *Living and Knowing* E. W. F. Tomlin; *The Danger of Words*, M. O'C. Drury; Roger Poole's *Towards Deep Subjectivity*, Phillip Rieff, *Fellow Teachers*, Theodore Roszak, *Where the Wasteland Ends*, Ian Robinson, *The Survival of English*, to mention several of very different approach. See also my *Human Hope and the Death Instinct*.

27

the bread of understanding. The intelligentsia has a special role in our democratic world as teachers of ideas, but every teaching is an emotional relation, a matter of loving your students. *It is a moving among them and taking part in their doubts in order to share together the adventure of common exploration of the unknown.*

Mental Seduction and Menticide. p. 206 (my italics)

It is this treachery we are faced with when Susan Sontag says that she 'recognises the truth' – but suggests that 'perhaps that is not always what we want'. Knowing is an act which involves us in responsibilities. Those who divide intellect from values and meaning are contributing to the damaging 'objectivity' rejected by Roger Poole:

> Objectivity contends that 'facts' have to be accepted if there is to be objective discourse. It is considered sub-rational to question the status of facts . . . The suggestion that some facts ought not to be facts is rejected as merely subjective. Objectivity insists that the facts he *accepted*. It takes as a premise that facts can be deployed in an objective, context-free way, even when the facts are about human beings . . . The facts of a situation have to be accepted for what they are: all subjective, ethical enquiry about the status of the facts under discussion is down-graded as sub-rational.

> *Towards Deep Subjectivity.*

Susan Sontag denies freedom and responsibility. Such intellectual treachery jeopardises our survival because it is a surrender of *responsible consciousness*.

Everywhere, even at the heart of respectable literary studies, there are persuasive vindications of fanatical immoralism. An American critic, George N. Wellwarth, writes thus about the first of the 'black' dramatists, Alfred Jarry:

> Jarry's greatest gesture of rebellion, however, was his alcoholism. There can be little doubt that he deliberately drank himself to death. Not long after his arrival in Paris, he must have made up his mind to make the supreme rebellious gesture of suicide. He chose alcohol as his medium because it was slow and because the immediate effects of alcohol enabled him to carry on his eccentricities undisturbed by the restraints of his own personality. Alcohol freed him from himself temporarily; eventually it freed him permanently from the whole burden of his life. In a way it was a heroic death, for it was a death for a cause, and probably it was not as pleasant a one as the casual drinker might suppose. It was certainly not an insane or unreasonable death. Rebellion as Jarry saw it was a quest

for total enslavement, which is death. Jarry chose to rebel against the ultimate by systematically destroying himself. In this way he conquered – paradoxically; for, having consciously sentenced himself to death, as it were, by deliberately bringing it on, he was able to be completely at liberty, completely contemptuous of all manifestations of social order during the period of life that was left to him.

The Drama of Paradox, p. 11

The new insights reveal Jarry's attitude as pathological. It is urgent for the Humanities to find the new truths which are emerging in the light of which (for example) suicide can be seen as a false solution to the problems of identity and meaning.

The problem is to escape from the habits of quantifying what cannot be quantified, such as persist in psychology, sociology and in thinking about man in general. As R. D. Laing has said:

> Persons are distinguished from things in that persons experience the world, whereas things behave in the world. Thing-events do not experience. Personal events are experiential. Natural scientism is the error of turning persons into things by a process of reification that is not itself part of the true natural scientific method. Results derived in this way have to be dequantified and dereified before they can be reassimilated into the realm of human discourse.
>
> R. D. Laing, *The Politics of Experience*, p. 55.

The first step, philosophically, is restoring the 'experiencing I' eliminated by Descartes and Hume. Philosophical anthropology sees man as the 'animal symbolicum', as a culture-bearing animal whose distinguishing feature is consciousness. This is the crucial problem behind cultural nihilism and our impotence in the face of it. Escape from our debasement is not a question of banning or suppressing. It is a question of being able to understand man's meanings and his need for meaning. Having grasped these as man's *primary* needs, we can unmask the falsities. We shall restore man's moral being to the world, and creative responsibility to our living.

Our struggle is against what Frankl calls 'homunculism'. In *From Death Camp to Existentialism* Frankl gives a harrowing account of the agony of preserving a sense of being human

29

throughout the dehumanising atmosphere of the concentration camp.** His conclusion was that man's primary need is not pleasure (Freud) or power (Adler) – but to satisfy his existential yearnings, his will-to-meaning, his quest for a sense of significance which can overcome the recognition, which haunts him, of his eventual nothingness. This accords well with the views of Cassirer and Susanne Langer, who believe that *man's primary need is to symbolise*. The will-to-meaning thus comes to the fore-front of our model – and this quest for meaning is bound up with our pursuit of authenticity, in which is found our freedom. This is the central emphasis of the new existentialism, and also of the psychology of Abraham Maslow, Ludwig Binswanger, and Rollo May. In this psychology, man's deepest fear is of his 'horror vacui' – of an emptiness of meaning within himself. His worst predicament is 'existential frustration', in which he cannot find his authenticity, in choice and action. He cannot find 'that which is within him, to become', Nietzsche's *potentia*. 'Release of instinct' or the 'satisfaction of the impulses of power' are no solution for these needs. When there is acute existential frustration, 'sexual libido' may become rampant, or a man may become seized with ambition, or an impulse towards violence.

In the Humanities it is our duty to emphasize that true solutions are cultural ones, that there are 'true' *solutions, and that it is natural* for man to pursue higher goals with vision and idealism. There need be no uncertainty, about the primacy of man's moral being, or his insatiable quest for meaning and values. The higher striving of man, as Maslow insists, is made plain in innumerable humanistic studies, of the kind which are able to find the subjective realm. There is, by contrast, no indisputable ground for those views of man which see him in the nihilistic dimension. To escape from this darkness, all we need do is to look at life around us, and go, in Husserl's phrase 'Back to the things themselves,' to look at the phenomena of consciousness.

** Originally published by Beacon Press U.S.A. Frankl's later books are available in Pelican Books, and in hardback from Souvenir Press. The book referred to here is now called *Man's Search for Meaning*.

Chapter Two

PHILOSOPHICAL ANTHROPOLOGY AS A BASIS FOR DISCRIMINATION.

We may be doing something for a long time, before we give it a lofty-sounding name. Today I might well describe my studies of children's writing as 'phenomenological', critical examinations of the phenomena of consciousness. This is not mere jargon, for it links the work both with a philosophical tradition (going back to Husserl) and with other similar work, on the meaning of art.

Philosophical anthropology embraces all those disciplines which are concerned with exploring human existence as *experience*. Marjorie Grene attempts a definition in her Introduction to Helmuth Plessner's *Laughing and Crying*, a book she calls a classic in philosophical anthropology:

> 'But, the reader will ask, what is philosophical anthropology? On the map of contemporary philosophy, it is hard to locate. As Plessner rightly insists about his own study, it belongs neither to any special empirical –ology nor to any special philosophical-ism. Philosophical anthropology is a philosophical study of the nature of man. But as Wilfred Sellars has put it, 'the aim of philosophy, abstractly formulated, is to understand how things in the broadest sense of the term hang together in the broadest sense of the term.' *Science, Perception and Reality* Wilfred Sellars (Routledge, 1963) Thus although a philosophical study of man may use psychology, neuro-physiology, physical and social anthropology, sociology, it *is* none of these. Nor does its perspective belong to any one philosophical school. In a way it resembles phenomenology, for its aim is description rather than argument, insight rather than analysis. But it entails no method of reduction, no intuition of essences, no claim to apodicity. Plessner's source in this little book, he says, is just 'experience'. And by this he means not the abstract units of sense or feeling of traditional empiricism but simply everyday experience in the most ordinary and comprehensive sense. The sciences of man, poetry, painting,

ordinary encounters of man with man; all this may be grist for the writer's mill. Whenever he can find it he will garner insight into human nature: in this case into that strange pair of human monopolies, laughter and tears.'

Laughing and Crying: A Study of the Limits of Human Behaviour. Helmuth Plessner, translated by James Spencer Churchill and Marjorie Grene. (Northwestern, 1970)

Philosophical anthropology is thus the study of man as a being-in-the-world, rather than as a natural object. It is not unlike the attention we give to man in the arts: but it is a rational discipline which looks at the phenomena of consciousness and the meaning of symbols and behaviour. It is, that is, real philosophy. As Ernst Cassirer says, the 'problem of man' is a landmark separating Socratic from pre-Socratic thought. The problems of Greek natural philosophy and of Greek metaphysics are suddenly 'eclipsed by a new question which seems henceforth to absorb man's theoretical interest: "What is man?" '

Socrates always maintains and defends the ideal of an objective, absolute, universal truth. But the only universe he knows, and to which all his inquiries refer, is the universe of man. His philosophy – if he possesses a philosophy – is strictly anthropological.

An Essay on Man, p.4

Husserl's whole point is that we should return to the original *telos* of Greek philosophy. And the wholeness of man must include intersubjectivity and the relation of man's inner life to 'encounter.' Maurice Friedmann says, 'The fundamental fact of human existence, according to Buber's anthropology, is man with man'. 'The "ought" is grounded in a conception of "authentic existence" '; it is 'essentially concerned with hearing and responding to what is over against one'. To talk of philosophical anthropology in this context is incidentally to point to a way of thinking which is also that of existentialism.

Buber's philosophical anthropology and the ethic based on it seems to subsist without the need for 'revelation' in the special religious sense of the term.

The Philosophy of Martin Buber. p. 122

32

This reference enables me to make it clear that the philosophical anthropology I am concerned with is as distinct as is Buber's from his religion, though not incompatible with it. Thus one may accept a philosophical anthropology, and its ethical implications, without being 'religious' in the special sense indicated by that 'revelation'. In philosophical anthropology it should be possible for agnostic, humanist, atheist, and believer (of whatever faith) to meet – on the grounds of observations of certain significant human truths, of a subjective kind, or what we may call a 'whole' kind. We have fallen into an unreal dichotomy, in which the objective scientist sees any recognition of man's subjectivity as 'mysticism' or 'teleology', so that my term 'philosophical anthropology' may even seem a threat to science itself. He seems to feel that if there is anything other than that which is observable and accountable on empirical lines, then science falls down – or at least, its pre-eminence is threatened. But this is only so, if science itself becomes obscurantist, and demands that all the phenomena of existence shall be accounted for by the 'objective' methods, data and concepts of positivist empiricism. This is to demand that all the complex mysteries of the universe shall be held as explainable by the one dimension, as 'nothing but'. The reductionist methods employed by physical science were devised for purposes of exploring the physical world: this science was *prohibited* from dealing with values, secondary qualities and consciousness. But there was no original impulse in this prohibition to deny that everything else exists! Yet this is what has happened, and not even all scientists see the fallacy of extrapolating from reductionism into a general philosophy. It is impossible to escape the feeling imposed upon our minds by the scientific predominance that the world of physics is the only universe we know. Science has stripped the world of meaning. It is not specialism that one objects to: it is the declaration that all phenomena must be explained by the one specialism: biology becomes biologism and psychology, psychologism. An intelligent scientist ought to know that the meaning of a musical symphony must be understood by the disciplines of the meaning of music (see Deryck Cooke, *The Language of Music*). No scientific description or measurement of the sound waves, or their quality, or the intervals of their mathematics can supplant our semiological analysis or our approach by analysis of symbols to that kind of meaning. Even the most complex 'scientific' analysis of the sounds or the twitching of our ears and nerve-centres could tell us nothing about the *Symphony*, and its creative engagement with chaos, as meaning. This musical work's structure and the relationships between its intervals and music 'shapes' may be as complex as a mathematical formula – and, in its conventions and dimensions as meaningful. But to *understand* it requires the proper disciplines of musical analysis, which is phenomenological, in that it must discuss modes of consciousness. Analysis of music can never be positivist. The mathematical relationship between the vibrations of a diminished seventh and a third may interest the scientist, but cannot explain the emotional meaning which bringing these two intervals together in a work of art can have for us. This meaning must be examined in terms of the language we 'speak' and hear, in the West's musical traditions, and of what the composer is 'saying', about (say) love and hate. So, too, the question of the difference between eroticism and pornography is not a matter of stimuli and body responses (to be measured by a 'penile plethysmograph'), but a question of meaning and human symbolism, in the dimension of the poetic. The growth of a child's moral capacities cannot be measured by an 'intelligence test' or other 'empirical' test, but only by an examination of his meanings and whole personality, and the relationship between the perceiving 'I' and the world he experiences.

Nor may we allow the scientist to have in the back of his mind the hope that 'one day' all will be 'explained' in reductionist terms. It is not our point that we cannot 'yet' do this: it is that we never can, since in such an ambition there is a confusion of dimensions. It is perhaps clearer if we take simple examples. It could be said to be 'scientific' to weight a footballer, see how far he can kick the ball, and see if, made to run twelve miles, he collapses. But if we say 'he has style', or 'he throws himself into the game so that he inspires everyone', this cannot be 'scientific', though it may be a recognised truth.

The point is made well by Maslow in *Towards a Psychology of Being*, an attempt to correct psychology, and especially psychoanalysis, by pointing to the fact that too much of it has concerned itself with sickness. Healthy psychology reveals more creativity. Human beings experience 'peak moments' during which the significance and uniqueness of their lives seems confirmed. Men cannot live without this sense.

> We are groping . . . towards the phenomenological, the experiential, the existential, the ideographic, the unconscious, the private, the acutely personal; but it has become clear to me that we are trying to do this in an inherited intellectual atmosphere or framework which is quite unsuitable and unsympathetic, one which I might even call forbidding.
>
> *Towards a Psychology of Being*, p. 216

This atmosphere often generates intolerance. Our journals, books and conferences, he says, are primarily suitable for the communication and discussion of the rational, the abstract, the logical, the public, the impersonal, the nomothetic, the repeatable, the objective, the emotional.

> They therefore assume the very things that we 'personal psychologists' are trying to change. In other words, they beg the question. One result is that as therapists or self-observers we are still forced by academic custom to talk about our experiences or those of patients in about the same way as we might talk about bacteria, or about the moon, or about white rats, *assuming* the subject-object cleavage, *assuming* that we are detached, distant and uninvolved, *assuming* that we (and the objects of perception) are unmoved and unchanged by the act of observation, *assuming* that all observation, thinking, expression and communication must be cool and never warm, assuming that cognition can only be contaminated or distorted by emotion, etc.
>
> p. 216

Maslow demands attention to the nonlogical, the poetic, the mythic, the vague, the primary processes, the dream-like. This is not to demand irrationality, nor to attack science. Other disciplines, or extensions of existing disciplines, must be developed to provide means of coming at the realities we wish to understand.

We must help the 'scientific' psychologists, says Maslow:

> To realise that they are working on the basis of a philosophy of science, not *the* philosophy of science, and that any philosophy of science which

serves primarily an excluding function is a set of blinders, a handicap rather than a help. *All* the world, all the experience must be open to study. *Nothing*, not even the 'personal' problems, need be closed off from human investigation . . . I am suggesting that we enlarge the jurisdiction of science so as to include it within its realm the problems and data of personal and experiential psychology . . .

p. 218

I also wish to extend the range of the Humanities, so that they recognise that their judgements and choices are essentially related to what science investigates. For instance, if biology discovers that man is primarily a symbolising animal, then it will seek to show that this symbolising energy has a function. This function will not in any satisfactory biology be judged in terms of 'evolution' or organic operation alone: but as something to do with human survival in the widest sense. One of the possibilities is that by using his symbolising functions man may come to discover both a greater sense of responsibility to the forces of life in the universe, and a greater freedom. Nothing could be less free than not surviving. Philosophical biology is the study of living creatures in this wider perspective.

Philosophical anthropology is an area of study within philosophical biology. It deals with man in his relationship to the world, to man, and to himself: it includes psychoanalysis, existentialist philosophy, existentialist therapy, and phenomenology, the study of the manifestations of consciousness. To recognise such a study is to indicate the problem of the nature of science. As Maslow says, science itself, insofar as it sticks to 'objectivity', may be actually a form of avoiding the whole truth. A more adequate science would take account of the kind of emphasis made by Adolf Portman in *New Paths in Biology* and by Kurt Goldstein in *The Organism*, requiring us to try to comprehend life-forms in terms of whole autonomous creatures.

The essential philosophical problem is indicated by Charles Taylor,* who said that to claim that Galilean empiricism *must* apply to human behaviour is not to pursue a logical conclu-

---

* *The Explanation of Behaviour*, 1964. Another useful study of the problem is Jan Foudraine's *Not Made of Wood, Quartet, 1976.*

sion but to make a speculative leap. Philosophical anthropology insists that the proper study of man involves a recognition of his consciousness. In the area of consciousness physical laws do not apply: we are in the real of the *Geistwissenschaften.*

It is worth reminding ourselves of the creative and conjectural nature of science itself as a manifestation of consciousness. Here we may usefully turn to Michael Polanyi's chapter Science and Reality, in *Science, Faith and Society* (p. 31):

> The propositions of science thus appear to be in the nature of guesses. They are founded on the assumptions of science concerning the structure of the universe and on the evidence of observations collected by the methods of science; they are subject to a process of verification in the light of further observations according to the rules of science: but their conjectural character remains inherent in them.

Furthermore, the interpretations of scientific data are made by 'a process of spontaneous mental reorganisation uncontrolled by conscious effort.' (*The Art of Scientific Investigation,* Beveridge). If a scientist supposes it is possible to be totally 'objective', he forgets himself. As Marjorie Grene indicates, though there is truth in science, its knowledge remains essentially 'contingent' – upheld by the guesses and opinions of 'those best qualified to judge'. There is 'nothing other than persons knowing', and our deference must be to a 'few great men' to whose learning we give assent, who created the structure we uphold as 'science' and 'learning'.

If science is only willing to see a world without the phenomenon of consciousness, then it cannot even 'see' the human mystery that is science itself!

Having insisted that science itself is rooted in a subjective basis – in people knowing – we may now insist on the authenticity of our own disciplines in the Humanities. In its dealings with what it believes to be 'facts', science rests essentially on subjective demensions in the persons who make up science. This subjective personal world is *our* area of research and study – and the human facts here have a reality which empiricism cannot study. The facts of culture more evidently belong

37

to consciousness and to meaning. That these 'facts' are only 'inward' does not mean that they are not real, or cannot be examined reasonably. But it does mean that they cannot be found by 'objective' disciplines. To be truly scientific about man, we need to recognise that even culture itself is a subjective reality, man's primary need for culture and meaning, his nature as *animal symbolicum*, is a biological fact.

The most complex of all organisms, man, has a special level of consciousness that distinguishes him from all other animals. But we are linked with the other animals by that 'something like' consciousness of which our consciousness is a special manifestation:

> Even our own mental life, is, as we well know, by no means wholly conscious; consciousness is one specialised expression of a much more broadly occuring phenomenon.
>
> Marjorie Grene

Psychoanalysis has explored these depths. The individual who is blind to man's inner life is denying certain aspects of reality. English, the custodian subject of the inner life, should be involved in combatting this blindness.

For the blindness has overtaken our civilisation: it is what Blake meant by 'Newton's sleep', indifference to the creative human spirit. As Marjorie Grene says 'nature comes to mean to us Galilean nature, in which the "primary life world" does not exist'. But we dwell in a life world. Not to recognise this is simply bad biology.

To find the category of life again is to find consciousness and culture – and so the dynamics by which man makes, transforms and transcends his material existence: all those aspects of being which science has excluded since the Galilean achievement. As Marjorie Grene says,

> we still stand . . . under the authority of the 'new science', and this was primarily the science of inorganic nature. 'Bits of matter, qualified by man, spatial relations, and the change of such relations' . . .

From the Cartesian ambition to 'solve all the problems which would ever confront the human mind', men had the ambition to create an exact science of life, of man, of society founded on the automatic manipulation of unambiguous, 'objective' variables . . .

But the result of this Newtonian ideal has been to turn scientific procedure into 'a mystic chant over an unintelligible universe' as A.N. Whitehead has called it. Nature has been reduced to 'an invisible billiards game played by chance against necessity' and our observation of it was limited to 'conditions, sad, passive and inert'. This has had disastrous effects on us as subjects who have come largely to 'know' the world, *and ourselves*, only in this dimension. If the world is like that, the only possible response is nihilism. *But it is not like that.* As Marjorie Grene says:

> we are in the midst of a new philosophical revolution, a revolution in which, indeed, the new physics too has had due influence, but a revolution founded squarely on the disciplines concerned with life: on biology, psychology, sociology, history, even theology and art criticism.

It is a revolution concerned to '*understand*', a revolution 'of life against dead nature'.

> The conceptual reform in which we are now engaged must restore our speech about the world to intelligible discourse and the world it aims at describing to significant and coherent form. Nature must be understood once more as the multifarious scene . . . a vast variety of forms, energies and events . . . of processes alive, active and striving . . .
> *The Knower and the Known*, p. 14

Our conception of a world 'without life' has led to a feeling that *we* too are 'without life' – without multifariousness, variety, sentience, intentionality, striving, creativity, or hope. This is embodied in our predominant present-day culture. So, 'reduced to the concrete' (Maslow), people have forfeited the future, like brain-damaged patients. By accepting the Galilean-Newtonian world, they have maimed their souls, and abandoned the future. Even the greatest achievement of imagination, of meaning, seem like sandcastles, to be swept away by the reality of the universe. But a new biology of culture would not find such nihilism justified.

We may take the first step towards a biological theory of

culture by looking at an amoeba, as one might in a science lesson. We need to see that there is another way of looking at the amoeba. This way is exceedingly difficult, because we are conditioned to look at things in those 'laboratory' ways which prevent us from seeing their wholeness, and the essential indivisibility, in universe and observer, of the creative dynamics of life as it exists and develops. To grasp this 'new' way we need new concepts and terms.

Polanyi distinguishes between 'attending to' (i.e. looking 'at' the amoeba) and 'attending from' – which is a way of *dwelling in* the amoeba by projecting oneself into it, imaginatively – the imaginative act involving one in feeling about the 'insideness' of the amoeba in terms of how one feels from the inside of one's own body. It is only 'by making intelligent use of our body' that we know ourselves to be in the body and not a thing outside, while our body is also the 'ultimate instrument of all our external knowledge'. The problem is to escape from the assumptions suggested by the habit of bringing the amoeba into the laboratory and making it react, passively. An amoeba lives, moves, senses, grows, by a dynamic of life, out there in the world. So, too, in a more complex way, do 'the birds in the trees'. We can thus begin to see a new dimension by which to study the way in which animals make creative use of their world. In the discovery of the essential 'centricity' of living creatures, we transform the universe into one in which life is at home, and no longer in an alien environment.

Plessner uses the term 'positionality', which means of organisms:

> that the body has an inner *core* out of which it has its parts and an outer aspect which is the aspect of that core. Its parts are peripheral relative to the centre, and the centre is the point of reference that makes the parts its parts. But neither core nor periphery in this context is simply spatial . . .

If the relation of inner and outer in the living body is not a measurable, spatial relation, how then is it perceptible or entailed in what is perceptible? How must we now look at an amoeba to see it in terms of 'the category of life' rather than as a dead thing?

Plessner is challenging the way in which by looking 'at' a thing in the old way, we *reduce* it.

> All qualities . . . resist . . . reduction: the physicist tells us how colours are produced, but he does not thereby exhaust or destroy the qualities of colour as perceived. Similarly, the neurophysicist tells us about the deeply-lying structures of the central nervous system which is the inner controlling agent of the organism's outward behaviour, but he has not thereby explained, let alone *explained away*, the quality of tension between inner and outer, the quality of being peripheral expressions of an inner core, that characterises life.
>
> *Approaches to a Philosophical Biology*. Marjorie Grene, p. 90 (my italics)

The traditional 'objective' way of looking at things sees them as 'objects' – and so tends to 'explain them away', by actual or theoretical dissection. Marjorie Grene says we should see them rather as 'subjects *having* such and such properties and parts'. This has an effect on the knower as well as on the known, for in trying to approach life like this, we discover ourselves as subjects. It also involves including those secondary qualities which the Cartesian tradition excluded out of distrust of the senses.

This is not to say that 'to be a subject having properties or parts' is to be a *conscious* subject. Consciousness doesn't come into it when we are looking at our amoeba, except our own. But in the light of philosophical biology 'something like' consciousness is present in higher living organisms. And when we come to human 'organisms' consciousness is a primary fact. We need to take into account the whole human creature as a being-in-the-world, whose consciousness is a manifestation of the unique self-activation and 'centricity' of all living creatures. Much of what is implied by 'mass' in such a term as 'mass media' is alien, since such a concept implicitly limits the subject to those aspects of man which can be exploited in a large group. The 'public' can thus threaten a nullification of man, by denying individual uniqueness. Man is also nullified by the 'social idea', as often found in politics, sociology, educational psychology, and the 'sociology of education'. All these nullifying generalizations, which can never find the 'fine grain of life', are put now into question as existentialism concentrates on the uniqueness of being.

Yet we still tend to approach such problems in traditional ways which imprison us:

> to see the problem solely in terms of physics versus introspection, of spacetime coordinates versus conscious feeling, is to see it still in terms of the Cartesian alternative which ... we *must* overcome if we are to do justice to our perceived, direct, undeniable experience of the quality of life ...
>
> Grene, *Approaches*, p. 90

The predominant 'scientific' view reduces that which transcends the organic back to the merely organic, so denying everything that makes life worth living, not least creative time. In *The Rainbow*, D.H. Lawrence struggled with this problem:

> 'No, really,' Dr. Frankstone had said, 'I don't see why you should attribute some special mystery to life – do you? We don't understand it as we understand electricity, even, but that doesn't warrant our saying it is something special, something different in kind and distinct from everything else in the universe – do you think it does? May it not be that life consists in a complexity of physical and chemical activities we already know in science? I don't see, really, why we should imagine there is a special order of life, and life alone –'

Frankstone's is the reductionist view. What he calls 'chemical and physical activities' are really only *ways of describing* certain aspects of reality which are capable of being described in such terms, in the *one* dimension. Reductionism as a method in science is quite legitimate for its purposes. But in the living universe, it cannot exclusively and finally account for how things are in their complex totality. Nor is it true that things simply *ARE*. The constant development of multifarious life-forms is still a great mystery, and they are moving forward in time. There are other dimensions: animals, for instance, have *moods*: birds 'enjoy' their singing long after its functional effects. The amoeba one is observing is of a different order of being from oneself, and cannot look at one in the same way: this alone indicates levels of being, so the 'system' of anything living is in a different dimension from that of a copper sulphate crystal, or even a 'DNA molecule'. The universe is full of order: all life strives: everything seems to move towards more meaningful forms.

Polanyi's discussions of the implications of the discovery of DNA are too complex to summarise here, except to say that he argues that the way in which life-molecules bring into existence so many meaningful combinations cannot be explained by reduction to physical laws. Biology cannot explain life by the working of physical and chemical laws. The 'pattern' by which DNA transmits 'information' cannot be derived from physical or chemical laws, and must be understood in other terms. If there are such different systems, and different dimensions in which they exist, then there must be different ways of knowing and describing these.* Moreover, in all knowledge about the world, *there is only persons knowing*, whose descriptions will involve their subjective life. Indeed, they only know the world by uncanny intuitive, subjective processes. The 'facts' of science are only upheld in living subjects who know and pursue them. The discovery of our involvement in knowing opens up new moral issues. As Polanyi says:

> Knowledge of participation, so firmly grounded, makes a clean sweep of the claim that in order to be valid, knowledge must be established objectively, without relying on personal judgement, And this restores our confidence in moral principles that are ultimately known to us by our commitment to them.**

In his *Personal Knowledge* Polanyi demonstrated that all knowledge is rooted in the participation of whole persons. Since science can only be something that scientists are doing it is not only false but immoral ever to suppose there is some body of 'objective' truth to which we must defer, or which can absolve us from participation in moral issues, values and meaning. Knowing of any kind involves a moral responsibility: the concept of 'objectivity' travesties this fact:

* Until these other ways of understanding life-forms are found, genetic 'engineering' is a highly dangerous activity. Obviously, Fred Hoyle's argument that life-molecules may exist in dust clouds between the stars is of major philosophical importance, since it opens up the possibility that life may be everywhere in the universe, seeking a home in which to fulfil its possibilities.
** *Proceedings of the Royal Society of Medicine*, Vol. 63, p. 975

For what I am attacking is a claim of science that is even more deep-seated than the ideal of explaining everything in terms of the world's atomic topography. Long before Laplace formulated the atomic theory of the universe, science had accepted the ideal of strict objectivity and claimed that its results were strictly detached, impersonal. And I have shown now that this claim is unreasonable and that its pursuit obscures the very essence of human existence. The facts of a stratified universe can be known to science only by a personal participation of the scientist, and this alone offers the grounds for securing moral values from destruction by a strictly objectivist analysis.

ibid. p. 975

Polanyi makes it plain that there are two dimensions, and the scientist knows this very well.

When Jacques Monod reduces Shakespeare's work to *nothing more than* the outcome of chance collisions of atoms it is implied that to account for all the positions of the atoms which generated Shakespeare would be a kind of 'truth' more important or significant than the works of Shakespeare, as they exist in the minds which respond to their meaning. The scientist recognises the higher dimension by talking about Shakespeare at all (rather than, say, Conan Doyle): but in his insistence that Shakespeare can be explained away in his physicalist dimension alone, we may detect a denial of the problem based on a hostility to the recognition of the very dimension of culture, a hostility to the existence of the creative consciousness; a denial of subjectivity. and the mystery of existence.

Polanyi notes that the scientist may believe according to his strict paradigm that he could explain the existence of his own family in terms of the collision of atoms or whatever. But he does not postpone his relationship with them until this is possible. 'No scientist refuses his affection to his family from disappointment because he cannot see them as atomic aggregates'. Yet today questions of meaning and value in public life *are* postponed until some 'objective' proof can be obtained, of a cause-and-effect kind, on which to base action – when, in truth, action must be based on moral judgements, in the whole dimension of human intercourse, and not postponed in the hope of some ultimate objective truth.*

* Examples are quantified behavioural objectives in education: intelligence

But, as Polanyi says,

the programme of the scientific outlook, as I have defined it, remains there. What varies is only the degree to which its absurdity is carried. In the case of Monod it is carried to the point of declaring triumphantly that science has deprived all value systems of their foundations, and solemnly subscribing to the consequent destruction of man's self-respect by a quotation from Nietzsche.

p. 976

Polanyi asks for us to build a truer world view, in which the grounds of man's moral being can be re-established. 'For this alone can save man from the alternatives of blind violence and paralysing self-doubt' – from nihilism, in fact.

The value of Polanyi's work is that it reveals some of the philosophical absurdities which lie behind a good deal of science when it turns to the 'category of life', and especially when it encounters consciousness, or the 'kind of consciousness' to be found in living creatures.

Happily, 'scientific' confidence has waned. What physicist today would confidently claim that 'we understand electricity'? In a scientific world in which it is possible to speculate that half the universe may be going backwards in time, such over-confidence seems absurd. Though we may believe 'H_2O' is all there is 'in fact' to water, it is now scientifically recognised that we know hardly anything about that most common of substances, and how its properties relate to its physical structure. When it comes to living systems, to say nothing of the higher animals, and above all man, the difficulties of understanding our universe become breath-takingly elusive. D.H. Lawrence was aware of the difference between reality as a whole, and mere scientific description, when he wrote his poems on water and electricity:

The Third Thing

WATER IS H_2O, hydrogen two parts, oxygen one,

---

and personality tests; decisions on truth and value in the sociology of education; and the attitude which claims there is no 'objective' test which can show the harm in pornography

but there is also a third thing, that makes it water
and nobody knows what that is.

The atom locks up two energies
but it is a third thing present which makes it an atom.

Storm in the Black Forest

Now it is almost night, from the bronzey soft sky
jugfull after jugfull of pure white liquid fire, bright white
tipples over and spills down,
and is gone
and gold-bronze flutters beat through the thick upper air.

And as the electric liquid pours out, sometimes
a still brighter snake wriggles among it, spilled
and tumbling wriggling down the sky:
and then the heavens cackle with uncouth sounds.

And the rain won't come, the rain refuses to come!

This is the electricity that man is supposed to have
        mastered
chained, subjugated to his use!
supposed to!

These poems not only indicate the mysteries denied by a strict positivist: they also point to the element in science discussed by Maslow: the impulse to reduce an ineffable mystery by a simple explanation, so that the immense powers of the universe are brought to seem as if we could, sometime, *control* them. It is not difficult to see how this attitude lies behind the ecological problem, and the whole question of man's plunder of the earth's resources: we are suffering from a lack of awe and respect, both in dealing with the outer world, and ourselves. Today, science itself is learning to develop more care in the face of 'the category of life'. The application of science will benefit by a greater sense of mystery, since this brings a sense of responsibility. One of the subjective aspects of science has been its implicit impulse to subjugate natural forces to man's intellectual will and power: the origin of this

46

impulse, in the light of Maslow's comment, perhaps, is man's desire to subjugate his own natural 'inner' life to his will and intellect. This was how Lawrence saw it: Ursula in *The Rainbow* puzzles over herself:

But the purpose, what was the purpose? Electricity had no soul, light and heat had no soul. Was she herself an impersonal force, or conjunction of forces, like one of these (she is looking at a plant-animal under the microscope)? She looked still at the unicellular shadow that lay within the field of light, under her microscope. It was alive. She saw it move – she saw the bright mist of its ciliary activity, she saw the gleam of its light. What then was its will? If it was a conjunction of forces, physical and chemical, what held these forces unified, and for what purpose were they unified?

For what purpose were the incalculable physical and chemical activities nodalised in this shadowy moving speck under her microscope? What was the will which nodalised them and created the one thing she saw? What was its intention? To be itself? Was its purpose just mechanical and limited to itself?

It intended to be itself. But what self? Suddenly in her mind the world gleamed strangely, and with an intense light, like the nucleus of the creature under the microscope. Suddenly she had passed away into an intensely-gleaming light of knowledge. She could not understand what it all was. She only knew that it was not limited mechanical energy, nor mere purpose of self-preservation and self-assertion. It was a consummation, a being infinite. Self was at oneness with the infinite. To be oneself was a supreme, gleaming triumph of infinity.

This passage suggests that we are very much influenced in our personal choices and conduct by the concept we hold of ourselves. Our view of the world (even of its *reality*) is always rooted in our subjective life. We cannot separate knowledge from the knower. Knowing is a form of being, and inevitably bound up with moral being. Accept these insights, and our culture should be transformed.

Ursula is struggling with the concept of existence held by the physics lecturer – that there need be 'no mystery' in our attitudes to life, and that everything can be described and regarded as the sum of its mechanical qualities and processes. The limited 'scientific' description of reductionism has been extended by this teacher to cover all reality. Ursula intuitively feels she must rebel – and so flies into the 'new reality' of love, to find the sphere of 'being'. Her pursuit is too intellectual, even there: belongs to much to the sphere of male doing and analysis. Our problem is to find the right kind of revolt.

Lawrence communicates how the scientific discipline itself can bring awe, and a deep sense of wonder and mystery. True science is thus an important cultural activity, not only bringing a respect for truth and for the mysterious complexity of existence – but also enabling an individual to ponder and develop a meaningful sense of his own being, his own existence in the cosmos. Pondering the existence and nature of a small creature gives Ursula a sense of how she must fulfil her being in the human sphere in a different way, and enables her to find a sense of relationship between her separate existence, and her union with all created life. This is an aspect of all culture, scientific or imaginative: it develops from the first capacities to experience separateness and union with the mother, who enables us to create our own identity, and is a meeting point between civilisation and the individual personality. Culture is our instrument of being-in-the-world: if it is deformed, our relationship with all things and beings is distorted.

In pondering our place in the scheme of things we must consider the influence upon our (possibly unspoken and unexplicit) philosophical anthropology of scientific theories and assumptions. These are still *hypotheses*, although the popular mind and the mind of the writer or 'Arts' man may accept them as unquestionable *truths*. One influence is unmodified Evolutionary theory. The inherent determinism in primitive Darwinism may be the product of crude biological concepts: there are perhaps more creative forces at work than mere 'survival of the fittest', and it may be that Darwinism, although basically a sound paradigm, may need radical revision. It is certainly full of logical absurdities (See *Darwin Retried*, Norman Macbeth, Garnstone Press, 1975).

However that may be in *science*, our thinking in the Humanities and in general, whether we realise it or not, is influenced by the impact of certain basic postulates of physics such as the Second Law of Thermodynamics on our attitudes. As Bernard Towers has said, the idea that because of the very nature of things the only possible ultimate future for man is annihilation has crept like a paralysis through our culture.

48

> Man as a whole is a dead duck. Significance must be sought, if at all, in analysis of the isolated individual – and this at a time when the individual, once he has arrived at his own most certain death, is looked upon as no more than a bag of bones undergoing the most probable process of thermodynamic decay.
>
> *Concerning Teilhard*, p. 94

In science, of course, such theories as those of evolution are continually under review, and may be seen in the context of biological time. The dinosaurs existed on the earth for 190 million years. In the popular mind they died out because they could not adapt to the changes in their environment. But such thinking is based on over-simplification. Dinosaurs and other prehistoric animals existed on earth for aeons, successfully, while by contrast, man's time on earth is as yet a momentary flicker. We might even say that man could not face the concept of surviving for 190 million years, while obsessed with the feeling that he may not survive one more century.

In biological time, what is surprising is the way in which forms of life proliferate: it is possible to look at the whole development of life in terms of the move forward, towards variety and richness. How did the flying creatures of prehistoric times develop their strange hollow bones, or the head protuberances which enabled some to have slender neck-muscles? To examine such questions in a positive way is to escape from the negative impact of the law of entropy, or strict Darwinian evolutionary theory. The scientist need not draw pessimistic human conclusions from theories which depend upon the 'survival of the fittest', because he sees the struggle to exist in terms of species spreading themselves out in order to triumph over the limitations of the environment, or adapting themselves in various ways, in order to proliferate in the vast orchestration of life. By contrast, writing in the Arts often assumes that life is a 'failure', and this leads easily toward giving assent to the 'end of civilisation'. To the scientist these are open, exciting questions about mysteries they revere: only in the Arts are they 'solved' by pessimistic and crude answers which promote futility.

What we are talking about, then, is the impress of natural scientism upon the popular mind and the Humanities. This may well be a matter of taking over from science as the one uncontested authority certain theories which seem to confirm a wilful tendency towards pessimism and nihilism. The appeal of such an approach lies in implicit over-simplifications of the problem of existence – as by seeing ourselves as machines without volition or responsibility. Masud Khan, for instance, says in his essay on *The Case Against Pornography* that man has tended to think of himself as a machine since the Industrial Revolution. Thus, reductionist theories from science confirm the ordinary man's mechanistic thinking about himself, in a society which tends to reduce him to a mechanism. So, too, some theories of biological development confirm a functional attitude to existence in a functional society, such as is criticised by Gabriel Marcel in *The Philosophy of Being*.

The effects on man's feelings about himself are discussed by Marcel:

> Travelling on the Underground, I often wonder with a kind of dread what can be the inward reality of the life of this or that man employed on the railway – the man who opens the doors, for instance, or the one who punches the tickets. Surely, everything both within him and outside him conspires to identify this man with his functions – meaning not only with his functions as a worker, as a trade union member, or as voter, but with his vital functions as well. The rather horrible expression 'time table' perfectly describes his life. So many hours for each function. Sleep too is a function which must be discharged so that the other functions may be exercised in turn. The same with pleasure, with relaxation; it is logical that the weekly allowance of recreation should be determined by an expert on hygiene; recreation is a psycho-organic function which must not be neglected any more than, for instance, the function of sex.
>
> p. 2

So, we find, in many spheres, this functional concept of man dictating political and other approaches to human life and leisure. The reference to sex and recreation is important: here positivism intrudes into cultural and moral issues, and we see how a 'scientific' model eradicates meaning and vindicates debasement.

This tendency is related to the ways in which an acquisitive, commodity-based society thinks of man. Marx examined the way in which the qualities of life, and human beings, are turned into commodities by an industrial-capitalist society, generating an 'alienation' and even a loss of confidence in active powers of mind. What is lost in such habits of thinking is the sense of meaning bound up with uniqueness in the individual life. Think of man as a functioning organism, or exploitable entity, in whatever sphere, and there is an immediate sense of meaninglessness, a loss of the intentionality towards the future in which meaning becomes manifest. If man is a mechanism, then he lives and dies only *as* a mechanism. He enters into his existence from the dust as nothing, his life is but a working machine going through its functions, and his death is a collapse of the organic machine. Opposition to the functional view of man has become an important theme in all existentialist thought.

Marcel speaks of the 'stifling impression of sadness produced by this functionalised world'.

> But besides the sadness, there is the dull, intolerable unease of the actor himself, who is reduced to living as though he were in fact submerged by his functions. This uneasiness is enough to show that there is in all this some appalling mistake, some ghastly misinterpretation, implanted in defenceless minds by an increasingly inhuman social order and an equally inhuman philosophy (for if the philosophy has prepared the way for the order, the order has also shaped the philosophy).
>
> p. 3.

It is this state of being 'submerged by our functions' with which the Humanities teacher should be concerned. As will be evident from my approach, this is not a question of religious belief: although Marcel himself was a Christian existentialist, the objection to the order and the philosophy applies, whether we have a religious faith or not. Human beings cannot exist without a sense of meaning in their lives, and this sense of meaning is explored through symbolism. But we live under the burden of a false symbolism, that of a functional attitude to ourselves, our bodies, our tasks. And the very structure of our lives, between factory, shop and 'living unit', has its own symbolism as an environment in which, by contrast with the traditional village, the functional paradigm of existence is predominant, even exclusive. Yet this non-meaning, non-spiritual environment is created by 'planners', who are then surprised by the results. People living in the huge concrete bunkers and spiritless wastelands created by functional thinking suffer psychic illness. Not only are their capacities for the higher meanings not met: the simplest needs for community and sympathy are not provided for either. Such living conditions evoke terrible protests – the inhabitants are still

51

human, and the only way they can express this is through violence or despair (See *Power and Innocence*, passim).

Both science and the Humanities must escape from this imprisonment, because such thinking tends to imprison us in that sadness, and that sense of 'ghastly misinterpretation', of which Marcel speaks. We know that what we believe is wrong, but we do not know how to escape from it. We are led to feel 'What is the good of it all?', as Teilhard de Chardin has pointed out. We need urgently to recognise that science cannot answer any serious questions about 'the point of life'. It does not even recognise that its belief in the universe 'running down' by Entropy is a deadly kind of metaphysic.

Strict objectivity is unable to tell us anything, since it is only concerned with *what is*. All science can yield is what Polanyi calls 'topography' – 'where the atoms are', and this answers no questions at all.

The revolution in thought to which I am drawing attention represents a way of studying man which *does* deal with the question of the meaning of life – without being a religion. It fills the gap, about which many are bewildered, between the rigid disciplines of science, which cannot allow any mystical or divine interference in the operations of matter and life-stuff, as it sees them, and religion today which, while asserting that 'Jesus lives' is being betrayed by attaching itself to facts. As Husserl urges, we must be philosophers as 'functionaries of mankind', dealing with *true being* (p. 17): we must fill the emptiness in our concept of existence by finding our inner realities.

The gap today is filled by blasphemies – the cult of the occult, the forfeiture of the self in group hysteria in 'pop', pornography, Karate, drugs, group violence, and various other forms of 'radical dissolution'. Analytical philosophy, in its bankruptcy, has betrayed us to irrationalism. Philosophical anthropology indicates a task begun with Socrates, indicated by Kant's fourth question 'What is man?' and as yet hardly begun: a rational, radical, intuitive, contemplative, open, sympathetic, loving pursuit of deeper insights into man's nature and the point of his existence. And hardly yet begun. Surely this is hardly the moment to refuse the challenge, and yield the Humanities up to nihilism?

52

Chapter Three

THE HUMANITIES AT THE CROSSROADS.

In 'the Humanities' we should be engaged in deep arguments between philosophies, taking responsibility for the true being of mankind 'toward a *telos*'. We should be exploring accounts of the nature of the world and of how we know the world; exploring in what ways there can be values and meanings in our lives, our knowing, our choices and acts. Unfortunately, even as philosophy departments proliferate, they refuse to undertake these tasks. Turn on a 'philosophy' programme on the Open University network, or attend a university philosophy lecture, and you will hear clever trivialities about terms and logic, but also the renunciation of the tasks of asking 'Who am I?', 'Why am I here?' and 'What meaning does my existence have?' – even of Kant's fourth question 'What is man?' Yet we cannot face the future unless we ask such questions. There seem to me two dangers. One is the avoidance of the problems. The other is the choice (which Mr. Falck seems to have made) to give allegiance to the essentially functionalist view of man behind the 'old' existentialism of Sartre and his following – a nihilistic view, because it sees man as 'waste matter', merely 'being-unto-death'. Man is impelled bravely to try to find meaning in his life, but forever doomed to failure in this: forever doomed to seek good relationship and love – but forever doomed to find this quest ending in sadism, masochism or indifference: with the added twist that it is in this quest iself, in becoming the object of another's regard, that one experiences the worst dangers of becoming 'objectified', becoming the object of another's gaze.

The view seems so 'brave': but it is, as I shall argue, a

schizoid view, and it embodies that essential element of self-defeat, of *huis clos*, of encapsulation, to which the schizoid is prone. In adopting this view, we are like W.R.D. Fairbairn's patient 'Ivy'. In this case-history Fairbairn delineates the schizoid individual who is attached to her negative and destructive elements, with 'ecstasy' – because her whole (false) being is constructed on the consuming joys of hating.*
By contrast we may consider the courage of a great creative artist. Mahler experienced the most terrible dread associated with the schizoid problem – of feeling there was nothing in the identity upon which to rely, while the world itself was bleak and full of menace and emptiness – yet broke through, broke out of the dreadful circle of encapsulation, and, with great courage, learnt to love – by listening to the creative and benign forces in the universe. With much pain and suffering, he *created* positive meanings, even without God.

This was a greater courage than that manifested in 'black' art, and greater than Sartre's (as a representative 'old' existentialist.) Some 'nihilistic' work is, by contrast, essentially sentimental, because it expresses only negative experience, only hate – and is determined to encounter neither tragic truth, nor the pains of loving, of exposing our human vulnerability, of encountering our desperate need for meaning. Samuel Beckett gloats on not-being, on not-beginning-to-be; sitting on the threshold of the womb, clinging to one's regression, not being born, declaring that no moving forward into creative time has any value. Beckett rejects all possible meanings. The only value is in *not becoming*, and in renouncing the determination *to be*, in declaring life devoid of Being and transcendence. Though some nihilistic work may have a value, as May suggests, by confronting us with the 'void' and prompting us to explore what we can set against it, much 'black' work, like Beckett's, does nothing of the kind. It recommends stoical paralysis, out of a sense of futility, and mocks all vision and creativity as 'pallid and artificial'. This 'old' existentialist 'courage' ends, as in Ted Hughe's *Crow*, in a

* *Psychoanalytical Studies of the Personality.* p. 27. 'Ivy' is discussed in 'On. the Nature and Aims of Psychoanalytical Treatment', *International Journal of Psychoanalysis*, 29 (5) 374-85 (1958)

silly joke, with much rather childish spleen directed at God, who does not exist anyway, as a 'cruel bastard' to man who is 'abandonné' (as if he has a birth-right but has been denied it as an exposed foundling). It ends in cults of suicide and obscenity, as if death and perversion were the only really reals.

In education today students encounter a doubly schizoid experience. Much in 'liberal studies' has gone empty and corrupt – even as it still seems a serious approach to human problems. It often takes on the seriousness of fanatical immoralism*. As the democratization of higher education proceeds, subjects become increasingly detached from their general humanistic meaning. Students are left with a desperate lack of the sense of relevance of their subjects to the central questions: 'What am I to do with my education?' 'How does my subject relate to civilization, to values, and to my role in the world?' 'What is the meaning of my life?' This often provokes a deep crisis, because the university has failed to provide indications of where answers might lie.

This crisis cannot be separated from the miserable fact that students have learnt their subjects in a schizoid way, split off, as an intellectual artefact, from living and existential problems, from meaning and *values*. A student writes of her work with me, 'I hope you realise what a difference it made to be allowed to *think* in supervisions, and to be given books to read which actually connected to our pre-University thoughts and comprehensions.' The next term, she says. 'I must be a sober Behaviourist . . . reading those glossy American textbooks' on social psychology.

I didn't think I was doing anything exceptional, yet, it seems, to discuss (with pauses in which I wondered if I was doing the right thing) psychology in relation to 'life' is 'different'. University teaching, my student told me, was mostly about what so-and-so said, while the student is not supposed to believe anyone, or adopt any particular point of view.

---

* An example is the pervasive study in school of William Golding's dogmatic and nihilistic *roman à thèse*, *Lord of the Flies* an eminently 'teachable' work whose perverse falsification of human nature was actually given the lie in life, by a catastrophe in the Pacific: the castaway children spent much of their time praying and led an orderly life.

The exigencies of an exam may mean that a student has to absorb material which she already recognises to be highly questionable.

But, besides this, the *content* of many subjects is schizoid, essentially nihilistic. This is true of Behaviourist Psychology itself: I do not reject all its findings, but ask for essential human qualities to be restored to its 'model'.

The concept of man essentially based on natural science lacks the intentional. If man is represented as a 'closed system of physiological reflexes or psychological responses to various stimuli' the openness of human existence disappears. In such science, in which 'values and meanings are nothing but defence mechanisms and reaction formations', there is a 'tendency to devaluate and depreciate that which is human in man'.

Frankl says students can hardly be blamed for their attitudes, because

> Nihilism has held a distorting mirror with a distorted image in front of their eyes, according to which they seemed to be either an automaton of reflexes, a bundle of drives, a psychic mechanism, a plaything of external circumstances or internal conditions, or simply a product of economic environment. I call this sort of nihilism 'homunculism', for it misinterprets and misunderstands man as a mere product. No one should be surprised today that young people so often behave as if they did not know anything about responsibility, option, choice, sacrifice, self-devotion, dedication to a higher goal in life, and the like. Parents and teachers, scientists and philosophers, have taught them all too long a time that man is 'nothing but' the resultant of a parallelogram of inner drives and outer forces . . . man becomes more and more like the image of the man he has been taught about.
>
> *From Death Camp to Existentialism* p. 109

Frankl realises that 'the gas chambers of Auschwitz . . . were ultimately prepared not in some ministry or other in Berlin, but rather *at the desks and in the lecture halls of nihilistic scientists and philosophers.*' In English students are *obliged* to swallow works without questioning their nihilism, or being given the opportunity to find resources from which to reject it. Many today have fallen into nihilism to such a degree that they feel life has no meaning:

There is . . . a practical, as it were, 'living' nihilism; there are people who consider their own lives meaningless, who can see no meaning in their personal existence and therefore think it valueless.

From Death Camp to Existentialism Beacon Press, p. 298

Some can see no moral objection to egoistical nihilism. Since there is no-one to whom to account for our actions or choices, on what can morality be based? If God is dead, is everything possible? Without transcendental realities, is there no basis for ethical choices? It is urgent to find some answer to such questions, if man is to survive, in the face of all his ecological, economic and social problems. Even Jacques Monod, a strict materialist, has said this will require a deep spiritual change in us. Unless we develop a sense of meaning and values, there can be no ethical basis for the effort to survive: the consequences Nietzsche saw will overwhelm us.

Frankl says 'education must be education towards the ability to decide'. But the 'old' existentialism makes us feel that all decisions are ultimately futile, so what is the good of educating people for futile decisions? Existentialism of the Sartrean kind has made it fashionable to denigrate all processes of love and interpersonal creativity, and to make us feel and act as if 'they' must always inevitably confront 'our' freedom. This Sartrean existentialism, as Marjorie Grene concludes*, 'provides . . . no adequate means of elevating the individual's search for freedom to the status of a universal principle.' (p. 145). It is an expression of 'an old despair', not (of) 'the new morality we may hope for.' (p. 149). This 'old' existentialism culminated in the recommendation of 'endless hostility', as Mary Warnock argues. It values perversion, by elevating criminals like Genet to the status of martyrs, and raising destructive nihilists like Sade to the status of admired moral heroes. In its endorsement of false solutions Sartre's existentialism could, as Roubiczek has pointed out, be used to vindicate an ethical position from which even the worst atrocities of Nazism seem to have their justification.**

* In *Dreadful Freedom*, now *Introduction to Existentialism*, University of Chicago, 1959
** *Existentialism, For and Against*, Paul Roubiczek, CUP, 1964. *Existentialist Ethics*, M. Warnock, Papermac, 1967.

Marcel complains that 'it is by no means a coincidence that Sartre's work offers the most glaring display of obscenities to be found in the whole of contemporary art'. The 'old' existentialism has become bankrupt, and Sartre's influence, cultural or political, can never help a revolution to come about. Sartre himself has spoken of feeling that his existence has become pointless. But the poison of his ethos lingers, though all we have left is the obscenity, bereft of its meaning-impulse.

The predominance of Sartre's nihilism in European philosophical thought has delayed urgently needed attention to the psychology of ethics and knowledge of a positive kind. It has also totally distorted the pursuit of a new and radical ethics such as could be found in the work of such thinkers as F. J. J. Buytendijk and Ludwig Binswanger.

Insofar as he is overwhelmed by the 'objective' sense of matter, even though he seeks transcendence, Sartre is really not an existentialist at all, but fails to find creative dynamics by which man may transcend himself. The 'old' existentialism fails to uphold the impulse, found in Nietzsche, to believe that the quest for transcendence is primary in man's existence. As Keller has said:

> Psychology is bad psychology if it disregards its own psychology. Nietzsche knew this, saying, 'he who does not *wish* to see what is great in man, has the sharpest eye for what is low and superficial in him, and so gives away – himself.'
> 'The Importance of Nietzsche' in *The Artist's Journey to the Interior* Erich Keller, 1965

Nietzsche himself was appalled at the possible effects of nihilism:

> The nihilistic consequences of our natural sciences – from its pursuits there follow ultimately a self-decomposition. In a frenzy of intellectual honesty man will unmask as humbug and 'meaningless' that which he began by regarding as the highest values in life. The boundless faith in truth, the joint legacy of Christianity and Greek 'logos', will in the end dislodge every possible belief in the truth of any faith.
>
> People have no notion that from now onwards they exist on the mere pretence of inherited and decaying values – soon to be overtaken by an enormous bankruptcy. I foresee something terrible. Chaos everywhere. Nothing left which commands: Thou shalt! Thou shalt not! There will be wars such as have never been waged on earth.

This prophecy has come true. The pursuit of truth *must* destroy values only when this pursuit is equated with 'unmasking'. There are other 'truths' about man and other ways of coming at them. For instance, from common sense experience, if not from Maslow's humanistic psychology, we know that most people find great satisfaction in being 'good': that their own well-being is bound up with their imaginative sense of what is going on inside others: that people care for others: that we are capable of love: that people seek authenticity within themselves: that people know their own fulfilment is bound up with the well-being of others: while everyone has a 'formative principle' within themselves. Human beings can be satisfied by the sense of meaning in life: they 'gain' by creative effort: they will experience great pain in the quest for truth and love, or even die for these.

There is a 'true self' in each of us and a true sense of our potentialities. There *is* something we may call 'ethical living', and from the collocation of millions of attempts at good ethical living values are created and upheld.

I am now pointing to a vast amount of psychological and philosophical work since Nietzsche, which is totally at odds with the whole trend of our culture. The biggest danger is that although this newly emerging pursuit of truth could lead towards a more adequate sense of values, fanatical immoralists are making a last determined attempt to create a nihilistic atmosphere in which this cannot be possible, *because of their fear of positive humanness.* If it is true that, 'Only the strong can love: it is the weak who hate', the weak would rather pull the whole house down on themselves rather than face being human.

Perhaps all a Mr. Falck manages to do in his Humanities 'hour' is to add to his students' problems by turning their attention towards a fascination with these empty gestures of a bankrupt culture – when they might have found a creativity in themselves, and in the culture of the past, by which to resist the creeping dehumanisation of our world.

This is 'mischief' indeed: one wonders what kind of help Mr. Falck can give, since his article placed no emphasis on that creativity of 'commitment' and 'growth towards their own shape' which alone would make literature worth having for his students? His approach, which is representative of a current fashion in liberal studies, is based on a model of human make-up which could not stand the scrutiny of the new philosophical anthropology. Yet those who take up such attitudes seem unaware that their implicit model of man seriously needs re-examination. They regard their position as more 'true' and 'realistic' than the old 'paternalistic' Christian, or 'elitist' views which they feel they have supplanted. But they can only believe this so long as they refuse to allow the original *telos* of Greek thought to intrude on their fashionable adherences. Husserl traces the whole crisis of modern scientific thought to the failure of our civilization to sustain this pursuit of *whole human truth*, and asks us to take up again its original impulse.* Once this goal is allowed, the views of such people as Mr. Falck are exposed as inadequate. Preferring to cling to nihilism, these people are displaying an anti-intellectual bigotry: yet today they are very successful, in creating an atmosphere in which further debate seems impossible.

As Daniel Boorstin has said, much present-day 'revolt' is combined with 'apathy of mind'. He calls these people 'Apathetes'.

> They abandon the quest for meaning, for fear it might entangle their thoughts and feelings with those of others and they plunge into 'direct action' for fear that second thoughts might deny them this satisfaction to their ego. Theirs is a mindless, obsessive quest for power. But they give up the very idea of man's need for quest. Instead, they seek explosive affirmations of the self.
>
> *The New Barbarians, Esquire.*

Boorstin, well aware of the psychological processes behind social change, sees that there is a fake revolt afoot, which depends upon the arousal of barbarous sensations at the expense of the genuine radicalism of true thought.

> They deny the existence of subject-matter by denying the need for experience ... The accumulated experience of books or of teachers

---

* *The Crisis of European Sciences and Transcendental Phenomenology,* Northwestern, 1970

becomes absurdly irrelevant. There is no knowledge, but only sensation and Power is its Handmaiden!

This requires a new sense of Time, which is both a separation from the past and a refusal to concern oneself with the Future. Survival itself is thus endangered.

> They deny the existence of Time, since sensation is instantaneous and not cumulative. They herald the age of Instant Everything! Since time can do nothing but accumulate experience and dull the senses, experience is said to be nothing but the debris which stifles our sensations. There must be no frustration. Every programme must be instantaneous, every demand must be an ultimatum.
> This movement from Experience to Sensation accelerates every day. Each little victory for student power or Black Power – or any other kind of power – is a Victory for the New Barbarism. Appropriately, the New Barbarism makes its first sallies and has its greatest initial success against the universities, which are the repositories of Experience ...

Their causes, says Boorstin, are 'the emptiness to end all emptinesses' – and it is towards this nothingness that some lecturers are urging on students, in the name of 'liberal studies'. The new Barbarism is not a new kind of radicalism; it has no specific content, no aims, and leads nowhere.

I am not asking that students should be kept in innocence. There is some value in putting students in touch with *some* nihilistic works, *among* others. As Rollo May says 'many ... contemporary dramas are negations and some of them tread perilously close to the edge of nihilism.' But May believes this to be a useful way of promoting the capacity to *care*:

> But it is the nihilism which shocks us into confronting the void. And for the one who has ears to hear, there speaks out of this void (the term now refers to a transcendant quality) a deeper and more immediate apprehension of being. It is the mythos of care ... which enables us to stand against the cynicism and apathy which are the psychological illnesses of our day.
>
> *Love and Will*, p. 306

Some nihilism presents us with the *Dasein* problem, the need to assert our hereness-and-nowness. The trouble is that many radical-chic approaches manifest no such positive impulse. They are more likely to promote cynicism, by undermining those ethical energies which are the basis of growth. As Rollo May says, 'the distinctive forms of consciousness in men' move towards 'self-realisation, integration, maturity'. In such implicit 'ethical statements' there is a hope whereby we may 'embrace the future'. *Dasein*-analysis demands of us that we *be something*. By contrast, the political aims of those who base their attitudes on 'scientific sociology' and homunculism betray the future by their failure to find *homo humanus*, whose primary need is to create meaning.

There is a sense in which individuals like Mr. Falck are heirs to a philosophical tradition of naturalism and scientific scepticism to which Freud himself belonged.

Polanyi links the fervour of the moral scepticism of the naturalist tradition with that homunculism of which Viktor Frankl complains as a threat to our need to cherish a sense of human dignity and potentialities. For the greatest threat is not hedonism, libertinism and scepticism, but the combination of moral scepticism with moral indignation.

Out of this morally fervent immoralism springs what Polanyi calls the 'armed Bohemian', and the Sadist revolution welcomed by the Sartres. Again, we have a schizoid response to a schizoid society. The schizoid individual, 'to whom the arts and other intellectual pursuits have a special appeal', tends to invert moral values according to two principles. Since love is so harmful, it is *morally better to hate than love*, or, by another logic, *since the joys of love are for ever barred from the schizoid, he might as well, immorally, give himself up to the joys of hating*. Winnicott's 'True Self' belongs to the area of 'being' rather than 'doing', and the ability to live from this essential sense of one's authentic being is created by 'togetherness' with the mother in the earliest years. Where this sense of self is not secure, the individual may come to depend upon some kind of 'false self organisation' as a 'strategy of survival', which may involve some compliance or comformity, and which feels mechanical and unreal. It is this 'false solution' which prompts moral inversions and hate, and may be schizoid. While the False Self organisation can be 'heroic', it remains False in the sense that it cannot realise the full potentialities of the individual and is in any case based on hate which cannot solve anything (see *The Masks of Hate*).

In an affluent, materialistic society, people suffer from existential neurosis because it is so difficult to find meaning. This is not a question of 'being happy' so much as of failing to experience tragedy, joy or an authentic sense of *potentia*. It is not that they are not 'free' or 'pleasured' enough, but that they suffer a deficiency of challenge and burden. Viktor Frankl writes:

> in the age of the existential vacuum, the danger lies . . . in man's not being burdened enough. Pathology results not only from stress, but also from relief of stress which ends in emptiness . . . Man does not need homostasis at any cost, but rather a sound amount of tension such as that which is aroused by the demand quality (*Aufforderungs-charakter*) inherent in the meaning to human existence. Like iron filings in a magnetic field, man's life is put in order through his orientation towards meaning. Thereby a field of tension is established between what man is and what he ought to do.
>
> *Psychotherapy and Existentialism.* p. 21

This need for moral tension cannot be satisfied by the ingestion of sensations, by acquisitiveness, or 'endless hostility'. It requires that we find causes to serve beyond ourselves, so that our capacities for 'being something' by 'intentionality' may be fulfilled, while our capacity to suffer or to have peak-moments may be richly experienced. In the dynamics of serving, or love, we may establish meanings which satisfy the *Dasein* longing.

This cannot be seen by those whose whole political and social stance is based on a limited rationalism, still infused with Rousseauism. As Polanyi points out, the effects of Rousseau's immoralism emerge from 'sceptical rationalism'. These consequences are a manifestation of a logical process which 'first ran its course through Rousseau's mind':

> He saw that the rationalist idea of a secular society imposed an unrestrained individualism, demanding absolute freedom and equality far beyond the limits imposed by any existing society. He saw, next, that such absolute sovereignity of individual citizens is conceivable within society only under a popular government, exercising absolute power. And thirdly, he anticipates the ideal of an amoral individualism, asserting the *rights of a unique creative personality against the morality of a discredited society*.
>
> *Knowing and Being*, p. 10 (my italics)

63

Here is the philosophical basis of the progressive concern with individual potentialities against the 'ethic of a discredited society,': it lacks, however, the sense of ideals and high values and cannot find objections to egoistical nihilism.

But what happens when political power becomes associated, as in Left-wing politics today, with such fanatical immoralism? What happens when Rousseau's position becomes sadistic, claiming to 'destroy everything in my heart that might have interfered with my pleasures', as it has in our 'liberated' culture?

We must restore the recognition of values to the study of man, which means opening up the subjective realm, not least those areas which are beyond access to the merely rational. Human actions cannot be explained without reference to the exercise of moral judgements, and attention to meaning.

One of the new tenets of radical thought is the denial of our cultural and intellectual inheritance. This involves an absurd denial that there can be achievement, and that civilisation depends upon it. We must respect our culture as the creation of human 'formative' dynamics:

> our cultural background is determined to a considerable extent by the influence of a limited number of men . . . Our modern, highly articulate culture flows largely from a small set of men whose works and deeds are revered and consulted for guidance . . .
>
> *Knowing and Being*, p. 136

Only chaos will come from the rejection of all values and meaning as a 'bourgeois hoax', the rejection of all values and meaning as 'elitism', in the fear of 'paternalism'. Even those who attack these things display implicit (negative) values in their very passion. Marcel points out that Sartre, while denying the existence of values, uses terms like 'good' and 'bad' to distinguish those who were willing to fight in the Resistance from those who fought in the Anti-Bolshevik Brigade. Our culture and thought are created by 'a few great men'. If this is elitist, why should we play *Don Giovanni* rather than *Poor Old Joe*? If values are mere class interests elevated into a morality, how do we discriminate even against the bourgeoisie?

Freedom demands a continual study of values and moral

choice, and of the way in which these are rooted in growth and relationship. They have their origins in what Sylvia Plath called, 'the wonder and hurt of loving'. There is today a new tradition opening up, of thinkers who are willing to explore the complexities of life, and especially to find love, meaning and values in the study of human nature – thinkers like Binswanger, as in his *Being in the World*. Marjorie Grene says of him that we have in his work an existentialist tradition which moves towards being able to accept 'encounter':

> Binswanger ... starting from Heidegger's *Daseinsanalyse*, distinguishes between two modes of human existence, the second of which Heidegger almost altogether ignores. He (Binswanger) distinguishes *existence*, as the *singular* being of the questioner, from *Dasein* (Human being) as *dual* being, as 'loving communion' (*liebende Wirheit*), a way of being which dispense with puzzlement and with fear.
>
> *Approaches to a Philosophical Biology* Marjorie Grene, p. 167

> We have to acknowledge the being of the individual as questioner *and* of the real relation of two individuals in mutual question and response.
> Man is a questioning being, the only being, as Heidegger has argued, for whom Being is in question. But he is also the only being whose questions can be put to rest through participation in the world of the mind – a world constituted by the union of persons in mutual understanding of the more than personal.
>
> *Approaches to a Philosophical Biology*. Marjorie Grene, p. 167

Marjorie Grene delineates a new philosophical movement which can see being-in-the-world, and intersubjectivity, as modes which can lead to a sense of meaningful existence, in a universe in which we are at home.

We may need occasionally to be faced with a degree of nihilism, that shocks us into confronting our nothingness. But such an experience should throw us back on encounter with others, into a dialogue in which we seek resources in that togetherness which is culture, and in love as a source of a sense of uniqueness and meaning. Dialogue, and thought, must take the form of responsible action. This dialogue, this responsible engagement with life, is not what the nihilists want.

Young people are striving to develop a 'True Self' and they are capable both of seeing how immature they are, and of being hopeful of maturing. This immaturity and its awareness of itself is an asset – a true naivety which exerts its own irresponsible but idealistic freedom. But there is the deliberate or calculated inculcation of immaturity: popular culture seeks to exploit the immature as a market. Professor Bantock and I find ourselves critical of 'pop' because it takes *advantage* of the immaturity we cherish, and undermines natural growth and self-awareness.

Our basis in making this resistance is rooted in intellectual vigilance. The amoralists or immoralists often claim Nietzsche as their own, thus revealing their essential illiteracy: Nietzsche himself diagnoses *them* and their hate.

The cardinal dilemma now, as it was for Nietzsche, is 'Can humanity and culture still be saved, or are both doomed to disintegrate and decay beyond repair?' (James Lavrin, on *Nietzsche*, op.cit., p. 91). The avant-gardists of education have settled for plunging more deeply into decay. They are too prone to confuse Nietzsche's 'beyond good and evil' with their own 'below good and evil'. As Lavrin says, such people 'often pretended to have found in Nietzsche a philosophical sanction for the very profligacy which he so frankly condemned.'

Nietzsche's emphasis on the orgiastic was not the recommendation of a relapse into barbaric sensuality. When all barriers were down, the human self was in danger of disappearing, or rather disintegrating, in the chaos of the amorphous pre-individual oneness. But this could be saved by the intervention of the opposite Apollonian element of *harmony, form, measure* and *individuation*: by culture and mind. The Apollonian should save man from sinking into his own pessimism. Nietzsche, says Lavrin, was a 'virtuoso in contempt for a commercialised age, in which everything was debased to a lower level'. He saw decadence as an escape from the problems of reflection, and the Apollonian:

> In the diseased or decaying body of Europe he concentrated on that process that threatened to dissolve and destroy the remnants of those cultural values what might still have been worth preserving. In one of his aphorisms he summed up the situation in these words: 'The whole of our culture in Europe has long been writhing in suspense which increases from decade to decade as in expectation of a catastrophe, restless,

violent, helter-skelter, like a torrent that will reach its source, and refuses to reflect — yes, that even dreads reflection.

Lavrin, p. 41

This plunge away from 'reflection' is overtaking education itself. Nietzsche assaulted the smug and prosperous Philistine with his abject 'pleasure for the day' and 'pleasure for the night' (all night 'X' cinema?). He saw that even the claims of the exploited masses hardly seemed to go beyond the aspirations towards universal Philistinism, fairly shared by all. (See 'The Last Man', in the first part of *Thus Spake Zarathrustra*, and Lavrin, p. 41).

If we are to achieve 'the ascending type of life', integration, and the realisation of potentia, we must still seek, as did Nietzsche, an antidote against nihilistic decadence, albeit not by his methods. Unless our work in the Humanities is devoted to this, there seems little point in having Humanities departments — which by their very existence should display a confidence in man and his future. As Abraham Maslow has said, 'much of what we now call psychology is the study of the tricks we use to avoid the anxiety of absolute novelty, with confidence and without fear': it is no function of 'liberal studies' to teach such tricks.

Any philosophy which leaves out either tragedy or joy cannot be considered comprehensive: we need 'peak-moments' of joy and ecstasy, while life continually presents us with tragic and painful experiences which draw out a fund of gravity and strength. These ranges have been excluded from too much of our thinking, and in this exclusion we have lost too much of our moral sense.

Chapter Four

THE SCHIZOID DIAGNOSIS AND THE 'BLACK' TRADITION

If hate is ceaselessly poured out into the world there is a serious danger of collective developments whose effects could be devastating. Political subversiveness, often operating in the name of love and humanity, may conceal psychopathological elements. 'Radicals' like Tynan sign letters to the press about freedom in foreign countries, while at home bent on debasing the human image, and humiliating woman in public, contributing to the erosion of values as certainly as those who harass and torture in 'repressive' countries. Meanwhile terrorist groups attack innocent people, and self-righteously claim their right to pursue their aims in this way, even when doing serious harm to their cause by their bombs, and killing and maiming members of the working class movement they claim to be serving.

The confusion becomes clear when the followers of nihilism and Oblomovism try to enlist Dostoevsky, who spent his life trying to become fully human. These critics seek to enlist him in anti-human movements, and make him the vindication for the cult of the intellectual gangster. The limitations of the (Matthew) Arnoldian or Leavisian position become evident when we come to such a work as *Crime and Punishment*. The problem of 'values' seems hardly relevant: one starts, as it were, too far down: one is at a deeper level – the level of not knowing whether one is a person or vermin. One starts, that is, from the schizoid position, the level of *not knowing what it is to be human*. Of course, to find oneself human is to achieve a value. But this is somewhere below moral values at the level of Arnold's concern and of Lawrence's dictum, 'the essential function of art is moral'.

We are in a sense floating above morality: but there is a deeper moral purpose, which is that of *beginning to be*, of becoming moral. Dostoevsky wanted to love, and to become truly human. Nothing is more moral than wanting to be human enough to be able to *begin* ethical living. Raskolnikov in *Crime and Punishment* seeks to become man enough to engage with the existential problem, through care and love: there is never any doubt that he wants to reach these goals. By contrast, some modern figures in the Arts have given up hope of being human, and do not want to be. They choose, like the Baader-Meinhof gang, "24 HOURS OF HATE EACH DAY" and their goal easily becomes suicide or chaos.

Ordinary morality belongs to the stages of development which come after the capacity to say 'I AM!' from a whole human self, so as to feel ruth for the first time. Ruth is that respect and concern for others, which can only come by 'encounter' and is an imaginative achievement.

Dostoevsky was no Oblomov, and his work is no mere act of subversion, moving towards schizoid futility or nihilistic destructiveness. In *Crime and Punishment* Dostoevsky makes perhaps the most tremendous quest in literature to find a sense of human identity, and the capacity to love, in order to make his way out of the schizoid predicament. It is ludicrous to imply that such a creative achievement was merely a response to an 'alienated' society, or to claim that Dostoevsky was 'destructive' in any way comparable with the 'subversive' art of today. As Janko Lavrin says, he demanded a 'continuous striving ... in the direction of that higher spiritual affirmation of life in which alone he saw a future worthy of human beings.'

There is a sense, admittedly, in which Dostoevsky may be said to relate to nihilism. As Michael Polanyi says 'The figure of Raskolnikov was independently revealed by Nietzsche in his tragic apologia of the Pale Criminal in Zarathrustra. But Dostoevsky undertook to explore the limits of nihilism, *in search of an authentic residue of moral reality*' (*Knowing and Being*, pp. 14-16 and 44). Dostoevsky's 'creative fury' represented a struggle to realise his own life-pattern, to find the true self and release its potentialities, through love. In this, inevitably, he came into conflict with a society which could not accept this growth.

Dostoevsky's work is revolutionary, in that it contributes to our sense of *what it is to be human*, so that we shall demand and seek to bring about a society which is able to receive and use our potentialities.

We can find through the insights of psychoanalysis the underlying phenomenological purpose in Dostoevsky's work. At the beginning of *Crime and Punishment* Raskolnikov's murder is, in the *symbolism* of that work, an attempt to feel real. The artist is seeking that sense of guilt of which a human being becomes capable at the 'depressive position'. This (according to Melanie Klein and 'object-relations' psychoanalysis) is that second stage in the development of the identity at which, having developed a sense of a whole self (and of the existence of a 'not me' against it) the infant becomes aware of the problem of the effect of his actions and impulses on the 'other'. It is thus a stage beyond the schizoid 'position' and emerges naturally as an act of imagination between mother and infant from the completion of this phase, into the 'depressive position'. By achieving this positive guilt sense Raskolnikov is able to overcome a schizoid feeling of his own worthlessness, to find the capacity to love and to feel human. That is, in Raskolnikov is symbolised that achievement which all normal infants complete naturally in the first year of life: but it is a process for which the adult schizoid yearns desperately, because he feels he has never experienced it. How then shall we take the ethical implications of Dostoevsky's novel? While Dostoevsky's discovery of guilt and the ensuing remorse are magnificent in the art, in life we can hardly sacrifice endless old women victims to young men's need to go through a beautiful experience of repentant self-discovery. *The lesson of the novel is by no means to vindicate murder.* A primary consideration here is the right of others to live.

Raskolnikov makes what Sartre would recognise as a 'valid choice', from his own 'arbitration', claiming his own 'freedom,' '*making himself*' when 'society' has given him no sense of meaningful existence. Then is *society* to blame? Raskolnikov is virtually shown as devising his *own* morality by

70

action, and making his *own* choices without the help of prior rules or principles. But his act must be seen as making a claim to find the reality of love as a source of being, such as is known by most other human beings. It is an act by which he is asking (or, rather, Dostoevsky is asking), 'What is it to be human?' If such an art-question is carried out in life, the result may be a futile delinquency, a trying-to-feel-real by hitting someone or stealing, murdering, or setting fire to something. As a symbolic work of art it can have creative value: not least because it enters into the realm of shared values. By his *symbolising* energy Dostoevsky was *completing a process in himself* – the discovery of concern, which involves a higher recognition of the existence of others. This was a way of completing a process which failed between himself and his mother (not between himself and 'society'), and so between him and his world. To act this out could yield no solution: it can only be solved by symbolism.

To Raskolnikov the old woman 'was' his mother (although she was not): to Dostoevsky the old woman was a *symbol* of his mother (or female parental imago), Raskolnikov a *symbol* of his impulse to attack and destroy this imago. To kill by 'acting out' in life would have been unethical in the extreme: to *fantasy* such killing in a work of art is by contrast 'ethical', since it is a path to the discovery of the universality of love. The process of finding the other and the world is an *imaginative* process and must be solved in this realm.

Dostoevsky was one of those writers who, like Kafka, are working not from the experience of being 'real and alive' but from being *unable to fell convinced that one is real and alive*. He was struggling desperately to feel real at all.

Dostoevsky was aware that the problem of feeling real was bound up with the question of feeling guilty, the need to 'attach the sense of guilt to something'. He needed to experience that anguish of guilt and concern by which we find 'the other' by imagining their feelings.

Much of today's cultural delinquency may be seen in the light in which Winnicott sees crime:

> in the more serious and more rare antisocial episodes it is precisely the capacity of a guilt-feeling that is lost. Here we find the most ugly crimes.

Of great importance here is the consideration of what constitutes symbolism and what does not. While we need to see the meaning of 'ugly' crimes, we must not accept the ugliness as 'beautiful'. We may understand the *meaning* of criminal acts but we must still see the acting out as unethical, because it hurts or destroys others. It may be an attempt to complete processes which have never completed themselves in infancy, towards an adequate relationship with the world: but ethical principles should not allow this at the expense of others. The falsity is in the confusion of fantasy and reality, and in the blank inability to find the other as he really is, in himself, and respect his integrity.

Where an individual cannot find a real sense of his relationship with the world, he may rob, murder and take part in perversions. He may then confess these acts, and thus move further toward a more meaningful relationship, because in confession he moves further into the realm of culture as a meeting point between separateness and union. If he creates a genuine work of art he may contribute to our culture. But his acts and confessions may also do serious harm, by corrupting others, seducing them into nihilistic modes which 'do not really belong to them', and spreading hate in society.

One of the serious dangers here is the supplanting of true symbolism by 'acting out' in which others are equated with hated objects, as in malignant perversion. Culture depends on a three-term relationship between the self and others that includes symbols that operate, like play, between one person and another. Many modern works break down this system. Dostoevsky may have begun with a symbolic *equation* in which the attack on the old woman (*equalling* the object) was necessary to him. In a film this might have remained acting out. Through the creation of the novel he achieved a *three-term* relationship in which the art came to be the embodiment of *symbols* capable of being used between his ego and his internal world with its internalised objects, and between himself and his external objects. By such an achievement true 'creative reparation, could be achieved, and schizoid dissociation over-

72

come. He achieves the 'three-term' relationship, and by such immense creative struggles was also able in his life to escape gradually from his gambling, and to become capable of love. *By becoming capable of symbolising*, Dostoevsky fought his way out of schizoid dissociation and impotence to become able to use symbols and to perceive a meaningful world. If he had stayed at the level of 'acting out' *equation* modes like many modern film-makers he could not have developed. It is thus absurd to use Dostoevsky to justify false solutions in which individuals 'give themselves up to the joys of hating'. It was these very false solutions from which the great Russian novelist sought to escape, into the capacity to create meaning.

As Kasanin points out in *The Language and Thought of Schizophrenics*, 'the schizophrenic individual may be one who has not completed certain processes, and is not yet able to symbolise.' He is often fixed in 'concrete thinking', and (as in our schizoid culture) to be fixed to the concrete is to be incapable of finding the future. Because of this confusion his acts may be unethical. If Dostoevsky was ever guilty of extreme 'acting out' of an equation-kind in life, as by committing the rape of which he was accused, then such an act can be seen only as a lapse into dissociation. We need to commend Dostoevsky for his creative struggle to discover 'what it is to be human', rather than endorse those lapses in which he became less than human.

For the fashionable avant-garde, however, a rape would bring Dostoevsky into the acceptable stature of the 'intellectual gangster': he could be placed in an honoured niche alongside Genet, and the anti-heroes of a hundred bad films. Sartre has elevated Genet to the status of martyr and saint, because of the courage of his false solutions. The courage is undeniable: but the essential substance of the identity achieved is 'false male doing', based on mental rage and hate.

The question of 'inner contents' is a crucial one. The problem is clearly a schizoid one for Sartre: inner emptiness must be filled with 'bad thinking'. But because he has no secure sense that can be based on the assertion *sentio ergo sum*, this inner stuff can never be trusted. His 'inner contents', though used to sustain identity, seem to vanish as they surge up from within. So great is the inability to rely on 'inner resources' that there is no faith even in the intellectual system that he constructs. To Sartre that form of excretion which is thought, converted into language as it is given out, may poison us if it is not kept 'fluid'. The meanings which are constructed by intellect alone have no roots in a felt security of being, but have to be continually remade by activity.

> As language may solidify and kill our thoughts, so our values may be solidified if we do not subject them to a continual process of breaking down and rebuilding ...

Iris Murdoch discusses his first novel, *La Nausée*. To Roquentin, the protagonist:

> the 'I' that goes on existing is merely the ever-lengthening stuff, is gluey sensations and vague fragmentary thoughts ...

That is, the 'I' of the False Self is excreta. Because this is 'bad' it has to be expelled. But the excretion brings the threat of a loss of inner contents. The image is of an 'I' which is made of 'doing'. The deeper fears are obviously of another possible 'I' which is mere being, so weak as to threaten loss of identity when the individual has 'given out'. Yet he must.

There is no solution, for the act of giving itself threatens dangers of 'emptying' oneself, while *not to give out* is to try to live *in* the excreta – in the sphere of intellectual hate, in the fragmentary construct, split off from one's whole existence and so 'pure'. So Roquentin hopes that

> 'A moment will come when the book would be written, would be behind me, and I think that a little of its radiance would fall upon my past. Then perhaps through it I could remember my life without disgust ... I should be able, in the past, only in the past, to accept myself.'
>
> Quoted by Murdoch, p. 15

The act of excreting inner contents in the form of thought and books becomes 'radiant' in that it creates a world in which it seems possible to live. Yet even this world is as fruitless and evil as the world of the flesh from which escape is sought.

As Marcel points out, the 'materiality' experienced by Sartre is not an 'abundance of being' but 'fundamental and absurd contingency'.

> Nausea is, at bottom, the experience of contingency and of the absurdity which attaches to existence as such . . . existence is unmasked at the root, bereft of its seemingly innocuous, abstract, categorical mien, and revealed in its terrifying and obscene nudity.
>
> *Towards a Philosophy of Being*, p. 58

Marcel asks what could be further, than the thoughts of Roquentin, from the traditional vision of the over-abundance of being, which has haunted all the great poets? For them, it is something positive, a glory.

Roquentin reflects that 'superfluity was the only relationship I could establish between those trees, those hedges, those paths . . .'

> . . . each of them escaped from the pattern I made for it, overflowed from it, or withdrew. And I too among them, vile, langorous, obscene, chewing the insipid cud of my thoughts, I too was superfluous . . .

Like the schizoid patients in Laing's *The Divided Self* he fears that he may flow away, out of an insecure identity:

> I thought vaguely of doing away with myself, to do away at least with at least one of these superfluous existences. But my death – my corpse, my blood poured out on this gravel, among these plants in this smiling garden – would have been superfluous as well. I was superfluous to all eternity.

But Sartre does not *place* this attitude as schizoid. Instead, he regards it as a revelation. As Marcel says:

> Such is the revelation, the negative enlightenment. Mark this particular combination of words, for it is the clue to much of Sartre's work. It is because Sartre's enlightenment is negative that his philosophy is, in the last analysis, the philosophy of not-being. No doubt it may be questioned if enlightenment can be negative: to say enlightenment is to say light, and absurdity is opacity itself, is the contrary of what gives light. If there is any light in it, it can only come from myself . . . Sartre's thought is eidolocentric

75

This kind of self is a phantom spun from the negative dynamics of the self.

Sartre cannot find an identity established securely by 'creative reflection' in the family. To Sartre the very existence of the family is profoundly suspect – and here is influence has been disastrous. In England existentialism has entered psychotherapy through R.D. Laing and David Cooper, whose addiction to Sartrean materialism takes the movement back into negative paths. Laing's *The Divided Self* is an important work of phenomenology: the *Leaves of Spring*, of 'praxis': but in the end both offer solutions in terms of blaming 'society'. Laing and Esterson become popular not so much because they dared to examine the phenomena of intrapsychic and interpersonal reality, but because their solutions and their championship of the schizophrenic fitted the patterns and cults of fashionable subversion. We live in a schizoid society, in a state of decay. But is it true that the individual is a 'victim' of his family and society as Laing, Esterson and especially David Cooper, suggest? Aren't most human beings still marvellous products of 'creative reflection', care and concern, in the 'ordinary good home'? The individual labelled 'schizophrenic' may easily become a scapegoat or victim in the processes of mystification. But may the problem not be that his identity has weaknesses which emerged from the primary processes of encounter with the mother. He is therefore felt to threaten the rest of the family, who turn against him as a defence measure to protect themselves? The problem is thus a failure of psychic parturition, which invites counteraction. The problem is one of fostering *being*, rather than condemning 'them'.

Our freedom lies in discovering 'that which we have within us to become', towards transcendent Being. Thus, our freedom is by no means as absurd, or our passion as useless, as Sartre makes out. To Sartre, values cannot be anything but the result of the initial choice made by each human being. They can never be recognised or discovered.

'My freedom,' he states expressly, 'is the unique foundation of values. And since I am the being by virtue of whom values exist, nothing – absolutely nothing – can justify me in adopting this or that scale of values. As the unique basis of the existence of values, I am totally unjustifiable.

76

And my freedom is in anguish at finding that it is the baseless basis of values.'

In philosophical anthropology there are many sources of recognition of reality. All values, and the individual sense of rightness, are the products of 'encounter'. There is the capacity for concern, drawn out in the baby by the mother, through that imaginative-cultural exchange. Then, through the influence of the family, the individual is given possession of these values which, by naturalistic description, convey to him that there is something that may be called 'rightness', in this circumstance or the other, just as there is redness in a red flag, or beauty in the dancing of a certain ballet dancer. Of course, such values need continual revision: but it is absurd to pretend that they are not present in our lives. Sartre himself often uses the words 'good' and 'bad', but what possible meaning can they have in his philosophy?

As Marcel says, Sartre promotes a 'devaluation of truly human modes of existence', and the effect is morally nihilistic: indeed, Sartre virtually says with the schizoid, 'Good be thou my Evil'. All is futile and evil, and all that is left to the individual is the anguish of being aware of this.

Iris Murdoch points to Sartre's preoccupation with the viscous, in relation to 'emptying and filling'. His impulse is to leave the mess – the intolerable ambivalence and vulnerability – of real life in the body behind. Feminine element 'being', which is the life of emotion, must be denied, because one was once dependent upon a woman, and her feminine element left one weak. The world in us derived from the 'female element breast' must be denied:

Emotion as a real creative power, as part of a new experience, Sartre does not recognise . . . he isolates emotion from the world; it is an imperious infantile gesture, a check to freedom, a *comédie* . . .

Iris Murdoch

The same fears of revealing the essential ego-weakness lie behind Sartre's theory of language: insofar as we are understood our inner contents may be stolen and our identities emptied.

77

> Language is that aspect of me which, in laying me open to interpretation, gives me away – *le fait même de l'expression est un vol de pensée* . . . ('The very fact of expression is a theft of thought . . .')
>
> Murdoch, p. 66

The fear of 'giving' in Sartre is compensated for by the impulse of writing. In Fairbairn's terms this substitutes *showing* for *giving*. Sartre himself believes that literature is 'sick', because of a separation of the writer from life, 'which has shown itself in either a hatred of language, or an absorption in language for its own sake, &c.' The writer has now been 'forced back to a living contact with the world by being placed in "extreme situations"'. But this suggests that Sartre's is a schizoid solution, which attempts to find love by substituting hate, and finds a sense of being real in violence itself, in 'doing': and in *acting out*: 'confrontation' in hate.

What seems to be lacking, in Sartre's concept of literature is symbolic-creative engagement, from a whole self, with a whole world. To him the impulse is *not to integrate, not to discover the True Self in a real world*. The impulse is to purify by hate, as the purgation is also that achieved by splitting and denial. His 'freedom' is a freedom from life itself. Sartre wants to purge life of its stuff, and free us from whole being altogether. Life must be reduced to an intellectual scheme, to an 'inner content', but one which has been purified by being excreted and by being removed for ever from the threats of female element being. The chaos dreaded by Roquentin and Sartre is the ambivalence of being human. Iris Murdoch goes on:

> Sartre has an impatience, which is fatal to a novelist proper, with the *stuff* of human life. He has, on the other hand, a lively interest, often slightly morbid, in the details of contemporary living, and on the other a passionate desire to analyse, to build intellectually pleasing schemes and patterns.
>
> Murdoch, p. 75

Sartre wants to subdue life to the perfect schemes of pure intellectual hatred: hence his idolization of Genet and perversion (the erotic form of hatred).

If 'false male doing' ever stops, the identity will go dead: so we are committed to endless hate-doing. We can only live in continual intellectual and political paranoia, which, if relaxed, will allow implosion, and the collapse of ego-boundaries. *Mauvais foi* is *being untrue to one's False Self.*

Sartre pretends to assert the 'absolute value of the person', but without reference to 'female element being' or to the sum of moral energies released by the reparative quest for the True Self. His essential model parallels that of 'objectivity', and belongs to the same flight from life as reductionist science.

What Sartre can never find is that touch, in love, with a person, who is discovered as a person, and who can confirm one's existence. His only possible essential humanness is a depersonalized image of a 'partial object'. Hence the addiction of the Sartres to Mlle Brigitte Bardot, who matters only as a projection of a 'breast' detached from a person on which is fixed the attention of millions in the act of symbolic regression to 'simplification of relationship'. To them 'she' represents what the stream of milk meant to Fairbairn's schizophrenic patient:

> The case of a schizophrenic youth who, whilst evincing the bitterest antagonism towards his actual mother, dreamed of lying in bed in a room from the ceiling of which there poured a stream of milk – the room in question being a room in his home just below his mother's bedroom. This type of regressive process may perhaps best be described as Depersonalisation of the Object; and it is characteristically accompanied by a regression in the quality of the relationship desired. Here again the regressive movement is in the interests of a simplification of relationship; and it takes the form of substitution of bodily for emotional contacts. It may perhaps be described as de-emotionalisation of the object-relationship.
>
> *Psychoanalytic Studies of the Personality*, p. 14

The sex-bomb is the same kind of schizophrenic symbol. She looks like a woman, but is in fact concocted out of 'pseudo-male doing'. Relationship with such a projected image brings none of the messy problems of emotional and bodily relationship and being, as with a person who has to be recognised as having value in her own right. This view of sex is one to which Sartre can offer no alternative nor can he to the the attitude to other people, that they are there 'to satisfy our requirements', prevalent in our culture.

Bentham reduced man to a 'bundle of appetites feeding themselves according to a mathematical formula'. Freud, the advertisers, and the commercial servants of our technological ethos concur. We find ourselves in the midst of a revolution of moral inversion, into which the population at large is being conditioned, not least by the arts and entertainment, but also by the critics who vindicate it and the philosophers who endorse the trend.

Marcel prophetically said of Sartre, 'Everything suggests . . . that his views will harden still further.' Recently Sartre has been reported as supporting Maoist violence, though he does not share Maoist theory: what could be more treacherous to the mind, to 'authenticity', to humanity? Those he shows most concern for are the terrorists of the Baader-Meinhof gang.

From a position of 'schizoid superiority' and pathological disdain, the avant-garde proclaim their godlike situation as being above morality, and thus above all normal responsibilities. Anyone who challenges this amoralism is ridiculed. Throughout the arts we find variations of the cult of the intellectual gangster established by the Sartres.

A characteristic intellectual gangster was Georges Bataille, in whose life one can detect parallel forms of splitting and projection. Peter Lennon said in *The Guardian* (June, 1967):

> Bataille, like Genet, had a notion, perhaps not to be taken too literally, of the 'sacred' nature of crime, and the quasi-divine role of the criminal of true integrity – the one who has no wish to come to terms with society.
> The idea of the sacerdotal role of the criminal faced with repugnant legitimate society is very common in French criminals above the level of shoplifters – particularly those who move in Parisian literary circles.

The criminal is only seeking to establish his identity. His act is an expression of hope: Winnicott, discussing the significance of stealing in children, says they are only taking what they feel is due to them, or trying to 'steal status'. The schizoid individual, however, feels it is unfair that society should punish those who take to his desperate way, when he cannot have access to theirs. What is left out is that the criminal's way is pursued *at the expense of others*. Others are moral, and they respect other people. This is unfair, too. What seems intolerable and inexplicable to the schizoid is that in return 'society' should resort to the same hate-activity as his, so that people at large maintain their own feelings of being sane and good by projecting their own hate over the criminal.

In these attitudes there are also valuable insights: as Lennon says, French prisons are exceptionally horrible.

The affluence of progress thus comes under scrutiny by the schizoid, who cares only about finding what answers he can to the question, 'What is it to be human?' He perceives that side by side with complacent materialism is the horror of the primitive institution. To alter this situation, however, requires a deeper sense of human value than the intellectual gangster can supply. He merely inverts values and calls criminality 'sacred', while quite unable to have any vision of a higher sense of human value. His inversions have now poured out in culture – with evidently destructive results, as one may see, walking the streets of Paris, or reading the newspapers.

We cannot vindicate anti-social behaviour on the grounds of the unpleasantness of society's response to the criminal, however. The beastliness of a society's punitive system can be judged by our notions of human dignity, and according to our ethical values. But the anti-social 'protester' may be making an assault on human value, in the name of liberty. He may even be thriving 'psychically' on this attack. He and 'they' are both antihuman complements to one another; he may be locked in unconscious collusion with 'society' in a sadomasochistic clinch, whose end is his inevitable death and the erosion of democracy and values.

Yet to him it seems that to be engaged in countering hate by hate has its own 'purity'.

This explains the uncreative nature of Sartrean Existentialism. A form of Nihilism, its effect is to contribute not to creative change, development and human growth, but to a self-preservative, solipistic concern with 'one's own ego' (Simone de Beauvoir). Meanwhile, it provokes in response a *hardening* of the social status quo, rather than change.

Considered as culture, a great deal of the output of schizoid individuals has a parallel sterility.

The modes of dealing with the world of those who have gone over to nihilism are based on moral inversion, the substitution of hate for love, and the denial of all possibilities of 'being for'.

The contempt expressed for humanity in much black culture today moves in the opposite direction from Dostoevsky's quest for 'what it is to be human'. By such influences people are developing an apathy and indifference to values from which democracy may be unlikely to recover.

In psychoanalysis and the new existentialism we find a concern with human fulfilment and freedom that never loses sight of the formative creativity in all individuals, and cherishes the creative conscience that can yield a sense of meaning in life The patient under existentialist therapy is encouraged to listen, to hear what his own True Self may utter, by way of indicating his life tasks*. But the Humanities teacher, too, should know from experience what Marion Milner tells us from her therapeutic work: 'patients seem to be aware, dimly or increasingly, of a force in them to do with growth, growth towards their own shape . . .' She found in her work something for which she uses the term 'formative principle' – an energy which organises and is pattern-making, 'shown in a person's own particular and individual rhythms and style . . .' This is the sense of potentia, of which Nietzsche wrote. There may at times be destruction and chaos in this area of creativity. But Marion Milner sees these as attempts to break down and discard a false organisation – as a means of discovering a new organisation of the True Self (*In the Hands of the Living God*, p. 385).

It is this constructive element in the chaos of creative effort that is hidden or diverted by today's nihilistic culture.

Ours is at the same time a civilization in which it seems to many, perhaps to most people, that there is no time, and no encouragement, to listen for the voices of the true self. Here there are complex questions. If there is a 'true self' and a sense of potentialities how do we recognise those? How do we know the 'true self'? The answer is, somewhere between our own creative dynamics and culture as the embodiment of the pursuits of truth. If our sensibilities and cultural symbols are corrupted, we cannot work adequately on these crucial questions.

*See *Existential Neurosis*, E.K. Ledermann, Butterworth, and also the work of Viktor Frankl, and Rollo May, especially *Existence – A New Dimension in Psychiatry*. See also *Being-in-the-World*, Ludwig Binswanger

Chapter Five

POLITICAL DANGERS OF MORAL INVERSION

Perhaps the most startling aspect of the new and aggressive nihilism of our culture is the failure of intellectuals to see the political dangers. It seems clear from humanistic psychology that our political system depends upon love and the family, and upon that degree of maturity in the majority upon which reliance can be placed, for people to make choices: the 'democratic character'. The nihilists and fanatical immoralists talk a great deal about people being 'allowed to make their own choices'. What in fact happens, as false 'liberation' advances, is that people at large are increasingly exploited by huge media organizations, which market hate and nihilism, while the less stable minority becomes even more unstable. The consequent increase in instability in family and community life constitutes a menace to democracy in future decades. Few critics have recognised the essentially 'fascistic' nature of a brutal culture; though Masud Khan has pointed out how the exploitative dynamics of pornography deserve this term, while others have dwelt on the political dangers of a violent culture.

The pressure of nihilism has to do with a serious loss of confidence, the loss of a sense of meaning in life, and consequent disintegration of the personality. Leslie H. Farber calls ours the age of the 'disordered will', and Viktor Frankl tells us that 'we are challenged by the question how to maintain or to restore a concept of man that does justice to the humanness of man and more specifically to the one-ness of the human person . . .' (*The Alpbach Seminar*). Rollo May discusses our society as a schizoid one, in which individuals fly as a compensation into violence or desperate sexuality (see *Love and Will* and *Power and Innocence*). Nihilism, fragmentation, the loss of meaning, and moral inversions of a desperate kind are closely related, and belong to the crisis of identity and meaning in man's life. The great disintegrations of our time (like 1914-18) have behind them tensions and disintegrations of the psyche.

These psychological processes have political implications which we need to examine.

Loss of meaning is the clue to many forms of violence and political desperation. In *The Doctor and the Soul* Viktor Frankl discusses the meaning of love, work, and death. But ours is not a society which provides meaning in these spheres – especially for the young. As W.H. Allchin writes:

> I believe that in our own type of society most adults are denied adult social status, power and responsibility and this has its inevitable effect on the upbringing of children, and their attempted entry into society.
>
> *Young People*, pamphlet discussed above, p. 6

In our society, 'only a minority can attain fully adult status as citizens.'

> The lesser status of all others, living within a weekly or monthly intake and output of money, is disguised beneath the weight of millions of pseudo-choices and the welter of distractions which are heaped upon those labelled consumers.
>
> Thus the negative identity commented on by Grotjahn. No wonder young people cannot respect those men and women who settle for less than full adult status . . .
>
> p. 16

Democracy, says Dr. Allchin, 'implies a real sharing of power and responsibility . . . it is a process of decision-making which is shared, and where time is taken to enable those involved to work out a genuine consensus, rather than having to adjust to the arbitrary decision of one individual, which on the surface may appear as an efficient method. The process has to be real if members of the community are to grow and mature through it.'

The inner life of man has come into contempt, and it is into this situation that a barbarous nihilism is now pressing. The political dangers are serious, and are worsened by the pressure upon the community to resort to paranoid-schizoid solutions.

D. W. Winnicott asks, 'what proportion of anti-social individuals can a society contain without submergence of innate democratic tendency?' Democracy depends upon the maturity created by family care in the 'ordinary good home'. There is always a minority of unstable people, and bad homes. The psychopathological dynamics which emerge from these can always be exacerbated:

> Many parents are not ordinary parents. They are psychiatric cases, or they are immature, or they are anti-social in a wide sense; or they are unmarried; or in unstable relationship; or bickering; or separated from each other, and so on. The thing is, can society see that the orientation towards these pathological features must not be allowed to affect society's orientation towards the ordinary healthy human?
>
> *The Family and Individual Development.* p. 161

Winnicott makes clear* that one fundamental factor in the mental health that sustains democracy is that degree of maturity which enables individuals to bear their own humanness, and to be able to bear to be dependent. It is perhaps surprising to the lay reader that it requires maturity to be able to bear being dependent on others. But at the unconscious level human beings need confirmation, and must needs open themselves to others in relationship. To admit so much requires that we admit our needs for others, and that we may be hurt, if others let us down, or turn hostile. There is always a problem of trust. All relationships involve this risk. To be truly independent, we need to recognise dependence: the very fact that we have personal resources is bound up with our experience of the mother's love. There is no true independence without dependence: no social ability without love. But relying on others exposes our vulnerability, and our sensitivity, which is a female attribute: only if we can tolerate female element being qualities in ourselves and others are we capable of belonging to 'community'.

All inter-human 'meeting' thus raises, at the unconscious level, feelings about our primary closeness to the mother, who

* *Some Thoughts on the Meaning of the Word Democracy, The Family etc.* p. 155

taught us our first socialization and who helped us to perceive the world and relate to it. Thus all political issues raise the question of our feelings about the internalised woman of our primitive experience. All social and political issues have beneath them the problem of the fantasy woman of our unconscious life.

Once, as Erikson and others have emphasized, we were totally dependent upon a woman; this remains in our unconscious as a fearful thing, because she was imperfect, and might let us down. Moreover, since no mother is perfect, this woman has at times seemed to frustrate us – so she has a rejecting aspect. We hated her, perhaps, or hungered for her when she frustrated us, and thought baleful things about eating into her body. So, the 'woman' in our 'shadow', or unconscious, has an aspect of which we are terribly afraid. The phantom is further complicated by the Oedipus complex, in which we become involved in our parents' sexuality, and thus come to fear the mother's possible attack on us, in talion revenge.

Thus, everyone has a latent fear of the witchwoman, the cruel castrating mother, the mother who is prepared to reject us and let us die, not least in revenge for 'emptying' her body in fantasy. It is to this woman that we feel hostility, when we exert cruelty on woman in society, or deny her equal rights. It is this woman who is humiliated in pornography, triumphed over, stripped, 'eaten' (albeit visually) like an edible breast-object, her personhood denied; at worst subjected to rape or sodomy, to exorcise the dangerous internal regions of her body. In Jung the anima or animus, the shadow of the other sex in us, may become malignant. The malignant anima is an especially troublesome force. She lies at the root of many political dynamics, and her phantom presence explains many of the darker proclivities of human beings, not least when they react in fear or rage: she is present in rape, in crime, in war, and in cultural depravity.

Commercial culture can exploit fear of this woman, in perverted and violent books and films, like those of Ian Fleming, in his 'James Bond' myth. (See *The Masks of Hate*)

Winnicott believed that one way of avoiding this fantasy woman is to put oneself under the care of a male dictator. This, he believed, explained

the tendency of groups of people to accept or even to seek actual
domination . . .
This impulse was

> derived from a fear of domination by *fantasy woman*. The fear leads them
> to seek, and even welcome, one who has taken on himself the burden of
> personifying, and therefore limiting the magical qualities of the all-
> powerful woman in fantasy, to whom is owed the great debt. The dic-
> tator can be overthrown, and must eventually die: but the woman of
> primitive fantasy has no limits to her existence or power.
>
> op.cit. p. 165

The effect of such processes is to make people feel *safer*. And
this may be applied to other collective processes. Following
Jung, Marie-Louis von Franz speaks of how, from fear of the
unconscious 'shadow', men can give themselves over to collective hysteria. Such collective false syndromes are likely to be
exacerbated at a time of low morale, and of economic-social
collapse. When existential frustration, already severe in the
kind of society Allchin describes, is deepened, to be human
becomes so intolerable that 'dependence' cannot be borne.
Out of fear of inner emptiness, individuals feel they will be
overwhelmed by the internal fantasy woman who stands for
their dependence on another. Their internal 'shadow' or unconscious reminds them of their existential emptiness and
nothingness. The hunger to exist in a meaningful way
becomes exacerbated, so that people feel there is within them
a hungry 'mouth-ego', threatening to eat up all around them,
even the world itself. The false self, with its combination of inclinations to be conformist or violent, can be collectivized.

Whole societies can experience such feelings, and are then
likely to move towards 'false solutions'. Cultural nihilism, pornography, occultism, and the drug-cult are all false solutions.
Love reminds people of their ambivalence and dependence,
and so is unacceptable: hate offers a greater appeal, because it
seems to offer an escape from dangerous love, and from our
weak and mixed nature. Hate offers that 'pure' appeal of the
'logically stabler state of complete moral inversion' of which
Polanyi writes.

Here we need to take account of two further dangerous
dynamics, of a paranoid-schizoid kind: *splitting* and *projection*.

If we become afraid of our love-needs, and of our inward emotional life, at a time of existential emptiness, we may fear that the badness in us may spoil the goodness. The 'dark thing' that 'sleeps in us' may seem to overwhelm all possibilities of solving our problems. The fantasy woman may turn black and bad, and overtake us, or annihilate us. Winnicott argues that when, to escape this possibility, men put themselves under the dictator who 'acts for her', she is exported from their inner life, and absorbed into the dictator, so she can be safely 'controlled' in him, and everyone feels relief.

But there is another way in which our blackness and hate can be exported: by projecting them into others, to whom we turn hostile in self-defence. We may seek to keep our goodness 'pure' by throwing the badness out of ourselves and 'planting' it in others. We do this to some extent, with the fantasy woman, who is 'exported' in pornography. Indulgence in this prepares the way for the next step in collective hate in defence against the phantom woman, as in Germany in the thirties.

How is this problem of paranoia and splitting relevant to the Humanities? Isn't it a very rare psychological problem? While we behave in a normal rational way, immense resources are diverted to external manifestations of paranoia; consider, for example, the cost of erecting, testing and maintaining the defence rockets of the west. These represent the most pathological manifestation ever created, of man's fear of what man might do to man. The paranoid insanity built into the ballistic defence system is discussed by Dr. Robert Daly. A rocket technician whose case-history he discusses believes that the future of the world depends upon both American and Russian engineers maintaining their rockets at the highest efficiency. He identified with the technical spectres – 'his ultimate definitions of self, the world and the meaning of his activities would be founded upon an unconditional commitment to technique'. Since the technical spectres were world-destroying, there was no future, while 'the personal sacrifices which he made in the face of the mighty forces which he was helping to perfect transcended any merely human concern.' (*The Spectres of Technicism, Psychiatry*, Vol. 33, No. 4, November 1970.)

This devotion to the end-game hangs like a poisonous cloud over all our lives, and has its effect on our deepest feelings. One deeply disturbing manifestation of it is the growing indifference to the welfare of children. The paranoid-schizoid syndrome in our world and its politics is associated with a growing failure of faith in the future. This is the phenomenological explanation of deliberate attacks on children, by terrorists like the I.R.A. and Arab 'liberators'. The same psychological dynamics may lie behind the unprecedented level of baby-battering and cruelty to children. In *Culture Against Man* Professor Jules Henry discusses the paranoid-schizoid phenomena of the war game:

> The Great Fear resembles a true obsession: like all obsessions its perceptions and anxiety-reducing measures transgress the bounds of reality: fly in the face of facts; have widely ramifying, unanticipated consequences; and, most important, are self-destructive in the long run.

The results of this paranoia in America, he says, are paralysis of thought; the tendency for the national character to have 'a fearfulness and a tendency to acquiese'; the accumulation of useless masses of 'classified' paper at universities: the failure to trade with the Soviet Union; and the over-dependence of the economy on preparation for war. Corporations engaged in defence, according to Professor Henry, make profits of up to 238% and 802% on investment, and absorb the major investment and energies of the economy.

Some manifestations of the reliance on schizoid hate as the basis of Western identity are strangely inverted. The executives of the Rand Corporation, producing missiles and weapons, are advertised as being 'the Renaissance man type'. Yet they represent an élite of death:

> Inasmuch as they are engaged extensively in the manufacture, deployment, and fantasy of death, it follows that they are the élite of death, and that what is maximised in our culture is the goal of death. The seerlike insight of Freud has therefore proved correct for in *Beyond the Pleasure Principle* he assumes a 'death instinct' that drove men ineluctably towards death. My only difference with him would be that while he thought the impulse to death was instinctive, I believe it culturally determined . . .
> Henry, ibid, p. 108

Professor Henry here strikes on an important truth: there *is* an impulse towards death in man. But not an 'instinct': rather a dynamic that arises from the false solutions by which Western man tries to sustain his identity. Splitting and paranoid projection tend to manifest against man's realisation of his potentialities.

To discover greater human riches would require that we relinquish our paranoid defences. But could we bear *to be*? At the international level this would require some way out of the monstrous duality of a world split between Russia and America. It would demand the reduction of the pseudo-tension of this confrontation, and greater effort to talk and meet, and to behave in more human ways.

Our unwillingness to engage the problem of bearing our humanness could be the psychic flaw which means that man will not be able to survive. We know from history that individuals may be 'possessed' by negative dynamics associated with a malignant version of the anima or animus. They can also turn this negative dynamic outwards, and attack their own vulnerability as if it were 'in' others who are really innocent. This is the dynamic of fascism: and of racism and pornography.

Winnicott's analysis of the psychological dynamics of dictatorship must make us doubt hopes that 'Nazism can't happen again'. Such developments of collective psychopathology are always possible, because of the tendency to shrink from the pain arising from recognition of the origins of our adult behaviour in the primitive depths of infancy.

Erikson draws attention to the problem of our fear of the female element and the realm of 'being':

> Historians and philosophers recognise a 'female principle' in the world, but not the fact that man is born and reared by woman. They debate principles of formal education, but neglect the fateful dawn of individual consciousness. They forever insist on a mirage of progress which promises that man's (the male's) logic will lead to reason, order, and peace, while each step towards this mirage brings new hostile alignments which lead to war and worse . . .
>
> Erikson, *Childhood and Society* Penguin Books, 1965, p. 393-4

Man's refusal to see himself as he really is has an unconscious basis in his rejection of his 'regressed ego', the un-born infant within himself:

> namely, the individual's unconscious determination never to meet his childhood anxiety face to face again, and his superstitions apprehension lest a glance at the infantile origins of his thoughts and schemes may destroy his single-minded stamina. He therefore prefers enlightenment away from himself . . .
>
> ibid. p. 39

Erikson recognised that for all of us the schizoid problem is the essential one (though he does not call it that): it is a problem of our infantile *weakness*.

> Every adult . . . has once been a child. He was once small. A sense of smallness forms a substratum in his mind, ineradicably . . . the immature origin of his conscience endangers man's maturity . . . infantile fear accompanies him through life.

The fundamental human fears are of being interrupted, impoverished, losing autonomy, of being closed up, of being restrained, of losing outer bounds, of being left empty and of *being left* (left to go out of existence when not 'confirmed'). At the heart is the problem of meaninglessness, of no sense of being to set against nothingness. All these are much more profoundly explained and accounted for, in terms of schizoid problems of identity, than they are in Freudian terms. And in a schizoid society there is 'a search for environmental provision' which is exacerbated by a failure of 'caring' in the community*.

The psychological analysis of past dictators is important, to expose the schizoid elements in their influence. Erikson links Hitler's own personal struggle for an identity with his 'ruthless' exploitation of his nation's fight for a 'safe identity'. In Hitler's Germany, however, says Erikson

> the black miracle of Nazism was only the German version . . . *of a universal contemporary potential*. The trend persists; Hitler's ghost is counting on it
>
> *Childhood and Society*, p. 317 (my italics)

---

* Winnicott describes a series: ' . . . the mother's body, the mother's arms, the parental relationship, the home, the family, the school, the locality with its police station, the country with its laws . . .'

91

Erikson seeks behind Hitler's mask of 'sweet brown piping' a false image of his own mother whom he transmitted as his own appeal and promise to lead the 'family':

> the mother devoting herself to the cares of household and looking after her children with eternally the same loving care . . .
>
> (*Mein Kampf*)

The truth was that Hitler's mother was twenty-three years younger than her husband, who was a drunkard and tyrant, and used to beat her. Erikson examines the consequences of the conflict between the truth and the ideal in terms of the Oedipus myth. In the light of object-relations theory we might go even deeper, and assume that the Oedipus situation only became critical because of earlier schizoid problems, which sprang from the mother's failure to provide an adequate environment in terms of 'being' for the formation of Hitler's identity. Let us assume that there was a grave failure on her part to convince the infant Hitler that he was loved for his own sake, so that he neither had an integrated identity, nor an integrated capacity to relate to others or to the world.

Erikson says that Hitler had a 'pathological attachment' to his mother. This might have been an over-compensation for her failure to 'reflect' him. But 'pathological or not,' inherent in the relationship was a gigantic capacity to 'split':

> he deftly divided his mother image into . . . two categories . . .

– the 'loving, childlike and slightly martyred cook . . .' and the '*gigantic marble or iron virgin.*' Besides these there are several superhuman mother-figures in his imagery, 'guiding and cherishing him':

> 'Fate . . . designated my birthplace . . .''Poverty clasped me in her arms
> . . .'
> 'Dame Sorrow was my foster mother'
> Nature is 'the cruel Queen of all wisdom'.

Hitler transfers these splits in his capacity to relate to his relationship with the 'mother country'. He speaks of this 'beloved mother . . . the young Reich' who was in a tragic alliance with the '*Old Austrian sham state*'. The 'Goddess of Fate' sends him to war, while the 'Goddess of History's eternal judgements' will justify his acts. The young hero of *Mein Kampf* returns to free and elevate the captive mother. He creates a mother who directs him, and a mother who must be freed and recreated.

Thus Hitler's mission is to obey, serve, and control a colossal ideal object. Yet, while the mother appears at times playful, childlike and generous, at other times she seems

treacherous, and in league with sinister forces . . .

Erikson accounts for this in terms of the 'irresponsible and childlike' role attributed to women in German domestic life: but it might be better explained by the insights of Melanie Klein, Winnicott, and Fairbairn. Where the mother fails as object, there is a desperate attempt to supply what is not there – a reflecting myth-mother, an excessively ideal object. But since the mother has proved unreliable in reality, all the fears of an intolerable ambivalence, of talion retribution, of castration and annihilation lurk behind the object: a split must be maintained at all costs. The problem of the archetypal fantasy woman is exacerbated. The splitting is accompanied by paranoia, as Erikson indicates:

The Führer's relationship to motherhood and family remained ambiguous . . . ambivalence towards the maternal woman became one of the strangest features of German official thinking . . .

The fantasy woman must be kept under strict control because she is dangerous. The fear of weakness of identity exacerbates the fear of the fantasy woman, who has developed from fears associated with the original unsatisfactory woman in the protagonist of a collective infection. Such unconscious fear and hatred of woman can have terrible political implications. Millions of Jews were thus in a sense sacrificed to Hitler's mother's failure, and her 'bad' side. It is deeply disturbing to realise that the same psychic mechanism lies behind pornography and cultural nihilism. The deep fear of the phantom woman can turn, as between the Weimar republic and Nazism, from the expression of a pathological hatred of female element being, to submission to the great idolized Iron Virgin Mother. Both are methods of controlling her, and seeking an ever safer guarantee against fears of dependence, either on a mortal woman, or on the fantasy Woman of the Great Debt. The dictator, by indentifying with Mother Germany, also *limits her*. Here we can perhaps link the failure of German morale in the thirties with psychic problems inherent in their social pattern. In the patriarchal German home the parents tend not to be adults treating one another as adults of equal value.

> When the father comes home from work, even the walls seem to pull themselves together ('nehmen sich zusammen'). The mother – although often the unofficial master of the house – behaves differently enough to make a baby aware of it . . .
>
> Erikson, op.cit. p. 322

In Hitler these problems made him incapable of relationship. The fear of 'bad' inner contents made him a teetotaller who abstained from meat, coffee, alchohol and sex, for fear of poison and contamination in the inner world, and in his concern for 'purity'. He did not acknowledge woman as a companion until the bitter end, when he made Eva Braun an honest woman.

> Hitler carried this . . . ambivalence toward women over into his relationship to Germany as an image, openly despising the masses of his countrymen who, after all, constitute Germany, he stood frenziedly before them, and implored them with his fanatical cries of 'Germany, Germany, Germany' to believe in a mystical national entity . . .
>
> ibid, p. 331

The paranoid-schizoid dynamic is evident: danger is now felt to be coming from 'out there', not from within. The Nazi concern that their hate should be 'pure' was often expressed in terms which resembled adolescent syphilophobia and fear of sexuality:

> 'Alone the loss of purity of the blood destroys the inner happiness for ever: it eternally lowers man, and never again can its consequences be removed from body and mind.'
>
> Quoted in Ziemer, *Education for Death*, Oxford, 1941.

But the obverse is also manifest in the attitudes which fly to the other extreme in our corrupt culture: depersonalised sex is the obverse of compulsive avoidance of sexuality. Women can be controlled either by purification or vilification. 'The idealistic adolescent's imagery', says Erikson, 'is typically one of the purest white and purest black. His constant preoccupation is with the attainment of what is white and the phobic extirpation of everything black, in others and in himself.' Hitler's path was the adolescent one of obsessive black purity.

Hitler's horror of Jewry was this symbolism in action. Jewry was an 'emasculating germ' – the danger being described as a weakening infection and a dirtying contamination.

When the reality became undeniable, that the *sumpfmenschen* ('men of the mud') of Russia, of Jewry and of the democracies could defeat the 'pure', healthy, handsome, and obedient German armies, 'his irrational fury knew no bounds'.

In Nazism, the libidinous, sensual self was split off and projected over the Jews and hated: in our time it is split off and projected over the woman victim in pornography and hated. The psychopathological element shows today, in those who refuse to see, or to discuss, the elements of cruelty and humiliation in pornography.

One of the most frightening aspects of the processes of splitting and projection, especially when they are combined with fanatical moral inversion, is the development of a 'cool' tone in which abominable things are spoken of as if they were perfectly normal. In *Uncle Tom's Cabin* the Christian whites on the Mississippi steamers, even including clergymen, accepted as normal the snatching of children from their slave-mother's arms, and the selling of negro husbands or wives away from their partners, despite their lip-service to the family as the basis of the Christian life. A similar coolness obtains today, in film and theatre reviews, in which psychopathological acts, such as copulation in public, are commended as if they were a new dance, or conjuring trick. While offences to high ideals, and even to common decency, are perpetrated on the screen or stage, individuals continue to sell tickets, take in people's coats and umbrellas, discuss next week's church fête, or sell ice-cream – just as people went on discussing fashions and books, while old Jews were being forced to scrub the pavements, or men were being tortured to death in Nazi camps. The trend is the same, that 'Evil things may be done with a clear conscience.'*

We can examine splitting and projection more easily in phenomena in which we are not involved.

In South Africa many Christians believe that the inferiority of one section of the human race is justified on scriptural grounds. For them there is a clear division between goodness which has been put into God and Lambs, and badness which has been put into 'black men': the late Dr. David Stafford Clark quoted in an article in *Christian Action* some letters on race that had been sent to Canon John Collins over the years. A woman in Southern Rhodesia wrote that black Africans 'have been created unlike the rest of the human race, from pigs.' This was why their hair was 'crinkly' and they 'smelt like swine'. They were the descendents of the Sons of Ham – 'all of whom were cursed by God and evil in the sight of men.' She herself and 'all other members of the human race like her, had been created from sheep; among whom was the lamb who became the Lamb of God . . .' Another correspondent wrote:

> You know that God said, 'let us make man in our image, after our likeness.' Likeness of course means facial appearance. Adam was white, Noah was white, David was white, Jesus whom we call God's Son was white, the Queen is white . . .'
>
> *Christian Action*, Autumn, 1966

The violence of objections to sexual relationships between white and coloured people (embodied in the Immorality Act) in South Africa has its roots in this inability to tolerate the 'intermarriage' of good and bad, pure and impure, love and hate, black and white in themselves. Their goodness must be kept 'perfect'.

---

* 'Gentlemen, you may think this is cruel,' said Goebbels about the extermination of mentally ill children 'but Nature is cruel.' This, too, is the argument of the pornographer. The relationship of these arguments to natural scientism is obvious.

Any British man who fails to register some emotion of shame or revulsion at the sight of a nigger or a wog with a white girl (even if she be a street girl) must have a bloodstream of PISS

Ibid. p. 15

Here the link with schizoid fears of inner poison if the exported hate were allowed to remain 'within' is clear. If a black man, in whom you have put your hate, has intercourse with a white girl, in whom resides your purity as a Britisher, your goodness will be spoiled. Purity depends upon being a chosen 'lamb', opposing the contamination likely to be brought by a 'pig'. Ambivalence is intolerable. Goodness must be kept 'perfect', and the hate kept pure too: the sons of Ham must be kept out of any possibility of 'inter-marriage', even with the impurest lamb – because if the purity and hate were accepted as being both within the ambivalent self, the identity might perish. Racism thus attracts schizoid individuals who feel the question of the maintaining of purity to be a matter of life and death.

Paranoid organizations such as the Jehovah's Witnesses or the Ku Klux Klan presumably attract those who cannot feel real unless life is made into a continual struggle against 'external replicas' of the threatening badness which they cannot accept within themselves. An article in the *Watchtower* speaks of 'the urgency of knowing how to repel the attack of wicked spirit forces' because 'Demon activity appears to be on the increase.' Such matters are not taken as metaphors of inward struggle, but are believed to be literally true. They smack of the 'concrete' thinking of the schizophrenic; to them 'the Devil' is not a symbol, but an actual 'equation symbol': they feel his literal presence as Bunyan did. If individuals feel themselves suffering physical demonic attack they must be virtually suffering from psychic illness. If enlisted in the Jehovah's Witnesses, their sectarian belief merely endorses the dissociation, persuading them that these hysterical delusions are real, and at the same time cutting them off not only from reason, but also from any possible medical help.

The idea that disturbances of the personality are caused by extraneous forces could be dangerous, since it might encourage 'acting out' of disturbed 'equation' fantasies. If the

Church appoints exorcists, it must thereby confirm the paranoid-schizoid tendency to split-off and act out, attributing evil to Satanistic external 'agents'. Such obsessions with the 'occult' are really psychopathological, and need treating as mental illness. On the other hand, commercial culture, moving on from the schizoid phenomenon of pornography, now exploits the paranoid-schizoid appeal of occultism, as with *The Exorcist*, social regardless of effects.

'Deep down, the schizoid individual wants to love and be loved', said W. R. D. Fairbairn; but such understanding does not mean that we merely accept or tolerate the morality of hate into which the schizoid individual seeks to seduce us. The schizoid individual is likely to 'give himself up to the joys of hating', and this negative impulse can become a disease of the unconscious mind at large. It is this that proponents of cultural nihilism forget, and because of this blindness they, too, are willing to jeopardise the future. Hate breeds manifestations of splitting and projection which are politically dangerous, and the consequent lapses are desperate ways of avoiding the question of being human, and suffering the pains of responsibility to man. Because they are avoidances, they take on a life-and-death quality of fanatical devotion to false solutions, which must end in chaos.

Chapter Six

MAX STIRNER'S EGOISTICAL NIHILISM, CULTURE AND POLITICS

I have argued here that the underlying philosophy of our culture has become nihilistic. If we pursue the implications of nihilism to their ultimate conclusions, where do we arrive? Very few have dared to do this: Max Stirner, who published a book on this theme in 1845, was one who dared.

The ultimate problems posed by nihilism are examined in a book on this German philosopher, by Dr. R. W. K. Paterson, *The Nihilistic Egoist: Max Stirner.* (Hull University Press, 1971). Stirner grew out of the neo-Hegelian movement, and published his one important work under the title *Der Einzige und sein Eigenthum* – 'The Unique One and His Property'.

Stirner belonged to movements which Marx rejected as 'intellectual nihilists'. Following the nihilist logic to its ultimate implications, Stirner denied God and Christian values, the State's authority, and all traditional morality.

But he went still further, and denied all ethical obligations. In the face of nothingness he embraced nothingness, and he sought no commitment or ultimate responsibility, to man or the universe: 'What is the commonweal to me?' All that he was left with was – self. The self and the world were ultimately Nothing – but the Unique One 'makes Nothing his cause'.

Stirner's nihilism, then, is very different from existentialism and philosophical anarchism, which seek a new ethic beyond the present false or stale morality. Egoistical nihilism seeks no greater authenticity or better society as these do. Stirner simply seeks to reduce the world – the others – to objects for consumption. 'Let us not aspire to community,' he said, 'but *onesidedness.*' 'Let us seek in others only means and organs . . . For me no one is a person to be respected . . . but solely an object . . . an interesting or uninteresting object, useful or useless.' The 'other' is but an object to be consumed 'whose only relation to me is that of useableness, utility, use'. We can hear in every phrase of Stirner's the attitude to life of tóday's cultural nihilist.

It is possible, of course, to reject this view, in the name of love, if one is a Christian. But Stirner demolishes Christianity. Of course, in Christianity itself, there are those, like John Robinson, who are willing to let God go, and transcendental values too – to find ultimate meaning in the 'personality', and declare that 'in pure personal relationship we encounter, not merely what ought to be, but what is, the deepest, veriest truth about the structure of reality', (*Honest To God*). But the radical atheist, like Stirner, is untouched by this. He will not give himself up to such an act of faith. To Stirner, relationships 'represent no more than pragmatic investments, in which part of his substance is expended in calculation of a direct and of course profitable return', as Paterson says.

Stirner always 'exacts a realistic price for any partial concessions he has to make to the "other" ' – no-one has any claims on him or his property, and he does not acknowledge the existence of any other person. He is Nothing, in that if he dies he is easily replaced: he represents no manifestation of God, or the universe. He is as Nothing to Nothing. The only way of passing one's time is not by any creative intentionality over against time and space, but only by ruthless egoism, regarding everything and everyone as one's property, if it is possible in any way to make them one's own. Life is a pastime, merely, consuming time by 'creative Nothingness'.

This ruthless aetheistical totality of Stirner is deeply disturbing – and yet challenges us, to declare what, then, we do stand for: what then can we say in answer? This was his challenge to Marx, who declared in favour of *praxis* – man's creative engagement with reality. Stirner would ask, in the name of what? A myth of social existence, or the social good, or some common ideal which could easily be demolished, and shown as a mere cloak for disguised egoism, in each member of society? If we are truthful, egoism is the only reliable and

100

dependable way of living, because that is how (undisguised) men live anyway: this is Stirner's view.

We would be wrong to take Stirner to be the most existential of philosophers, or the most ruthless of the anarchists. It is easy to mistake his energy for a creative one: after all, he speaks of '*creative* nothingness'. Stirner may even resemble Kierkegaard so closely, that there is an almost 'doppelganger' effect. But in fact Stirner is only a 'kind of diabolical mirror-image' of the Danish philosopher of Dread. While Kierkegaard emphasises 'the choose-thyself may replace the know-thyself', Stirner declares 'Get the value out of thyself!' While Kierkegaard finds a new emphasis for ethical responsibility, Stirner merely moves from the transcendence of Nothingness to a 'creative Nothingness' that culminates in 'Egoistic Self-enjoyment'. As Camus said, 'There is no act of destruction from which Stirner will recoil' – and in the end, 'on the ruins of the world, the final victory of rebellion is celebrated by the desolate laughter of its egoistic monarch'.

Stirner affords a challenge to the 'old' existentialism. He represents the total encounter with nothingness: 'the existentialists need to acknowledge – in his unique one – the one finished, historical instance of that total encounter with nothingness from which they themselves have in the end recoiled'. The existentialists have clutched and clutched at some metaphysical and moral transcendent, says Paterson, 'to provide a meaningful foundation for their personal world, lest it be consumed by its own insecurity'.

For Sartre, man is nothing, 'a useless passion', and exists before he can be defined by my conception. To Sartre man's consciousness is identical with the individual's choice of himself as present to the world of his choice. By conscious choice he transcends himself. But Stirner too spoke of a 'finite, self-dissolving ego' that transcends the self it leaves behind, as 'a fresh moment of the future beckons'.

Yet Stirner's 'creative Nothingness' does not create the world in becoming conscious of it, in the sense the existentialist believes possible. Stirner's approach involves annihilating and dissolving the real world: the world is merely 'food' to the egoistic self. 'I am not Nothing in the sense of

101

vacuity,' declares Stirner, 'but the creating Nothing, the Nothing out of which as creator I myself create everything'. Rather than bear the dreadful burden of solitude and responsibility that the recognition of nothingness imposes, men will lose themselves in the world and let themselves be taken over by it, Heidegger believed. But Stirner went further towards an ultimate denial of all essences, ideals, God-given, mythical forms of delusion about the real nature of our 'abandoned' state.

So, while Sartre's existentialism strives towards constructing something, albeit by *doing* rather than *being*, with evident solemnity, Stirner's philosophy moves towards 'criminal frivolity'. To us he says, 'it is precisely what you hold *sacred* that I would not respect'. For Sartre, the self that is chosen has value only because it is *chosen*. The freedom which I am is the freedom to choose. Both Stirner and Sartre reject any role, or self, imposed upon one without choice. 'If this freedom is surrendered, the alienation which I suffer is at once a servitude and a petrifaction'. Both are thus led to a negative attitude to relationship. 'While I seek to enslave the other, the other seeks to enslave me,' says Sartre. 'The original meaning of Being-for-others is conflict.' For Stirner, too, 'there can be no relations, either for cooperation or of opposition, between individuals each of whom ultimately inhabits his own private and exclusive universe'. Both philosophers, says Paterson, work out a given pattern of *endless conflict*.

Sartre's lover 'does not desire to possess the beloved as one possesses a thing he demands a special type of appropriation'. But although the attempt in the end is doomed to futility, Sartre's is at least an attempt to find the existence of the other, however much it becomes an attempt to 'seize and reduce the Other's subjectivity'. At least in Sartre we find objections to this objectification of the person: to Sartre it is terrible to be reduced to a thing.

By contrast, Stirner's principle is to exploit the other: 'I do not allow myself to be disturbed in my self-enjoyment', he declares, 'since I practise a Terrorism of the Self which drives off every human consideration'.

The Unique One has purged his world of 'persons' and the

nauseous 'values' which persons exude (Paterson, p. 184). The Unique One's project can be completely carried through by an act of self-consciousness in which his world will be simultaneously depopulated and devalued.

'I want merely to be I,' declares Stirner. 'I think nothing of Nature, men and their law, human society and its lore, and I sever every connection with it, even that of language. To all the demands of your Ought, to all the pronouncements of your categorical Judgement, I oppose the 'ataraxy of my Ego'. (*Kleiners Schriften*). As Paterson points out, while the world inhabited by the Sartrean existentialist, by Heidegger's 'authentic individual', and by Stirner's Unique One may be essentially the same, they have different views of the way in which one exerts one's personal mode in it. To Heidegger, to live as an egoist merely enjoying one's status and possessions, is to be a 'fallen being'. To reduce others to objects is to Sartre inevitably suicidal. Moreover, for Sartre, self-realisation is doomed since man in his attempt to find himself by losing himself reveals himself as a 'useless passion'. But even in the 'old' existentialism, there is an emphasis on 'commitment' and 'responsibility'. From this position a new direction remains possible – and in the 'new' existentialism of Ludwig Binswanger we find a quite different mode emerging: an existentialism based on *liebende Wirheit*.

By contrast, the philosophy of the Unique One is a philosophy of *disengagement* – a refusal to become involved, even with those you enjoy. It is a philosophy of ultimate irresponsibility: there is nothing and nobody in Stirner's universe to respect. Such concepts as 'authenticity', summoning man to a high existential 'resolve', or of the recognition of 'concern' at the root structure of human existence have no place in Stirnean nihilism. 'Rootless and unconcerned, the Unique One traces the changing circles of his factitious identity in consultation with himself alone, and without reference to any ideal of personal 'integrity' other than the integrity which comes from refusing to be debauched by personal ideals,' says Paterson (p. 187).

Even the most pessimistic existentialists represent their situation in an alienated world as a 'predicament' which demands to be *overcome*. Authentic choice for them is a *solution*. 'Fundamentally, it is the truth of nihilism which has to be overcome, and it is the artifice of commitment which is his chosen solution.' Only in this can the existentialist achieve a solution to the *Dasein* problem.

The response of the nihilistic egoist, by contrast, *is* an artifice which 'reflects and carries forward' the *nihilistic egoism, 'gratuitously adopted in a world in which all responses are gratuitous, and consciously withholding meaning from a situation which it found to be originally meaningless'.* (Paterson, p. 188, my italics). The posture of the egoistic nihilist is thus an act of supreme treachery to man. Finding the problem of meaninglessness in the world, he plunges into a solipsistic answer which finds a meaning for *him*, in the embracement of disintegration and doom: but he eats *his* 'food' – and grows fat on the consumption of those he has made his 'property'. As Paterson says:

> the nihilistic egoist's original project of self-satisfaction can only be carried through in a world which mirrors his own disintegration.

Is it true (as Paterson seems to think) that existentialism, as one central mode of belief in our culture, must come to this conclusion: 'it is precisely in this world that, according to his own avowals, the existentialist's project of personal integrity is doomed'?

Fortunately, there are clues to the falsity of Stirner's position to be found in philosophical anthropology and its insights: and in the 'new' existentialism. For one thing, Stirner *used the language*, and writing itself represents manifestations of togetherness, union, communication, concern and values. As Paterson points out, Stirner is not strictly a solipsist, since *Der Einzige* is full of references to other egos, and he speaks to them in the first person plural: '*You* are not to me, and I am not to *you*, a higher being ... Let *us* aspire to one-sidedness.' The Unique One is not literally unique: it is a metaphysical entity with which he identifies. For Stirner to write a book addressing others was a betrayal of his nihilistic position itself. And, from this, an unwinding of Stirner's absolute nihilism must inevitably follow – since, once he implicitly recognises others in this way, Stirner's 'use' of them must impair their capacity to pursue *their* own integrity. Moreover, to write a book is to seek to persuade others, and thus to affirm purpose and imply values of the kind he denies: we may say, with Fairbairn, that deep down the schizoid individual yearns to love and be loved, and this betrays his nihilism.

Dr. Paterson is clear himself that Stirner is schizoid. His description of how Stirner's Unique One is born is a description of the emergence of a voracious schizoid 'libidinal ego':

> The vacuous, impenetrable self of the 'free person', who negates and consumes the world in the act of exploiting it, is the embryo of that 'creative nothingness' in which the identity of the Unique One is centred and from which he emerges to disembowel and caress the physical and social universe in which he alights.
>
> p. 52

The physical terms used by Stirner ('my food') have a physical undercurrent that manifests the 'mouth ego' of the 'unborn child'. The world is to Stirner a primitive breast, to caress and empty: a body to be scooped out. His fear of relationship as likely to lead to servitude and petrifaction is a characteristic schizoid fear (p. 179). His impulse to 'use life up' is a schizoid impulse:

> enjoyment of life means using life up . . . consuming it in the way that one uses a candle in consuming it . . .
>
> p. 180

Only to a schizoid individual would it seem that there is only a certain quantity to be 'used up' in life, or that one's manifestation towards life should display such a 'sucking impulse' (a diagnostic phrase used by Guntrip of the adult who remains psychologically a deprived child).

Stirner's whole way of seeking *autonomy* can be understood in the light of Laing's analysis of the schizoid predicament. He operates and creates his philosophy by 'false male doing', and intellectual hate: his real name was Johann Casper Schmidt, and his own identity seems an assemblance of fragments.

In reality, after writing *Die Einzige und Sein Eigenthum* Stirner settled down to an indolent, dilatory existence. The book was his single act of self-assertion: constructing a negative intellec-

105

tual system in which to exist. Stirner was indifferent to other personalities and circumstances. His was a not-life, with a not-philosophy: the implications for our egoistical-nihilistic culture, whose world-view so closely resembles his, should be taken. Stirner became boring and ineffectual: his future died.

Ernst Schultze (in *Archiv für Psychiatrie und Nervenkrankheiten*, 'Stirner'sche Ideen in einem paranoischen Nahnsystem') argues that Stirner's book exhibits many of the features of paranoid delusion – though it escapes psychiatric condemnation because Stirner is willing to extend to others the boundless egoistic irresponsibility which he claims for himself.

But Paterson admits that:

A case might well be made, then, that the self-absorption, the destructiveness, and the negativism advocated and practised in *Der Einzige und Sein Eigenthum* represent the conceptual expression of the paranoid schizophrenia suffered by the philosopher who was at once the book's author and its subject.

p. 18

It must be said, however, that to devise a paranoid-schizoid intellectual system, a person need not be 'schizophrenic': as Guntrip shows, there are many schizoid individuals at large, who are by no means schizophrenic, and quite able to carry on a normal life. Dr. Paterson pleads that we must not reject *Der Einzige* as a 'pathological tissue of obsessional fantasies'. We must make an unbiassed exposition and analysis of the contents of the book itself first. But the schizoid nature of Stirner's nihilism is, all the same of great importance to our analysis.

He was the only child of parents who were old, and his father died when he was an infant. His mother married an oldish man, and left him for several months when he was four years old. His home life consisted of several uprootings, and the parental roles were supplied by god-parents. His mother was mentally ill and totally incapacitated for the last twenty-four years of her life. His life is the record of a repeated failure to pursue any goal consistently or to form any stable and enduring relationship.

Stirner made two marriages – both failures. One day, dur-

106

ing the first marriage, he accidentally caught sight of his wife's unclothed body: from then on he recoiled from any physical contact. The second wife said she 'had neither respected him nor loved him'. He 'left no record of a single person with whom he established a relationship of mutual affection'.

All these details help to establish a phenomenological picture of a schizoid individual who had to hold himself together by whatever scraps he could steal. The philosophy seems to follow inevitably: 'Our only relation to one another is *usableness*, utility, use.' 'I am not an ego along with other egos, but the sole ego.'

Stirner speaks of 'creating himself' – and this is what the schizoid individual feels he has had to do. Since he has had to steal and create a factitious Self from fragments, he has no respect for natural creative processes:

'I think nothing of Nature, man and the laws, human society and its love, and I sever every general connection with it . . .'

To all of these Stirner opposed 'the ataraxy' of 'my Ego': hate.

If we accept Winnicott's views, that play is both the origin of culture, and the way in which the self develops, then we can see certain forms of thinking and culture as means by which a secure identity is established. But we can also see 'black' culture (and perversion) as desperate attempts to solve such problems when they have not been solved in infancy in the normal way. Paterson has a chapter on 'philosophy as play':

Stirner's attitude to the world-system, or system-world, over which he presides as the Unique One, is essentially that of the *player* . . . To be a nihilist, Stirner has surely well illustrated, is essentially to play at being a nihilist . . .

p. 310

This is not so much a moral comment, as a phenomenologically diagnostic one. We may link it with the analysis made by Robert Stoller and Masud Khan of the perverse forms of play in sexual deviance which have as their undercurrent the impulse to exploit and even annihilate the other. There is often in these a strange combination of 'acting

107

out' and frivolity. Many cultural perversions today belong to 'criminal frivolity' and tend to promote an impulse to annihilate the 'other'. The element of 'acting out' is seen by Dr. Paterson:

> Unlike the existentialist, the self-consistent nihilist – if he is Stirner's nihilistic egoist – settles, without guilt or recrimination, for a life in which he will accordingly do more than 'act out' the nihilistic identity which he has chosen.
>
> p. 310

The nihilist does not commit himself, and refuses to take anyone seriously:

> His choice of a nihilistic identity, within a nihilistic world, is neither privileged nor inevitable; but given this basic choice, the quality of *frivolity* with which it has to be willed and lived *is* inevitable. Since, in the last analysis, nihilism is the refusal to take anything or anyone seriously, it must also be the refusal to take nihilism, and the nihilist himself, seriously.
>
> p. 310

While the cultural nihilist today is applauded in his 'play', every week brings evidence that this nihilism is having its effects.

But if egoistical nihilism becomes the fundamental attitude to life purveyed by our culture, what are the political implications? Not only would a society 'in which Stirner's self-centred indifferentism becomes a generally held attitude' . . . be 'a society on the brink of dissolution', as Paterson says. But now his 'rootlessness, irresponsibility, destructiveness, and self-seeking' are becoming predominant in a world which has adopted Stirner's position towards existence, even if it has never heard of Max Stirner. This decline has a metaphysical significance, representing 'an experience of the apparent worthlessness of everything, of general futility, of profound and all-consuming meaninglessness'. Stirnerean nihilism thus promotes that 'longing for non-being' of which Saul Bellow writes in *Mr Sammler's Planet*.

The danger is that people may seek to arouse themselves out of apathy and anomie by violence, on the lines diagnosed by Rollo May. There can be collective infections arising from egoistical nihilism. It may well seem, as Paterson says, that Stirner's philosophy is too egoistic ever to become collective, since collectivity, even in destructiveness, implies submission to an ideal, and ideals are abhorrent to the Unique One. But we should ponder these problems carefully, when extreme right-wing organisations are operating among football hooligans and unemployed delinquent youth, some of whom have committed crimes dressed up in garments imitated from forms of 'creative play' in films like *The Clockwork Orange* and *The Wild Ones*.

At large, we do not have to look very far, to find the inheritance of Stirner expressed in attitudes to life. The pornographic magazine declares 'Let us seek in others only means and organs'; the *Penthouse* organisation, now worth £88m, rose on the maxim 'For me no one is a person to be respected, but solely an object.' Not least in the minority press, we find the assertion of Stirnerean egotism, 'I practice a terrorism of the self'. Reviewing Professor E. J. Mishan's book *Making the World Safe for Pornography* in *The Listener* Mr Alan Ryan wrote:

> He writes as an outraged conservative moralist who knows that some things just *are* decent, natural, proper, satisfying, and fully human . . .
> *The Listener*, 27 December, 1973

This is to say that 'I think nothing of Nature, men and their law, human society and its lore . . . To all the demands of your Ought . . . I oppose the 'ataraxy' of my Ego.' Mishan, Ryan declares, shifts from 'liberalism to the police state' by suggesting that controls are necessary, because we do not really want to lead 'dishevelled and chaotic lives'. As if to make his Stirnerean connection plain, Ryan replies that we cannot go back

> without interfering very drastically with what most of us presently want to do.

'I practice a terrorism of the self which drives off every human consideration'.

On what grounds are we to accept that there is no longer any difference between decent and indecent, natural and un-natural, human and inhuman? There are no grounds in the proper study of man, in philosophical anthropology, for relinquishing such values. A powerful group of journalists, it is true, have asserted such a relinquishment in the last few years, and they exert a powerful intolerance of opposite points of view.

They thrive in the atmosphere of positivism, because in its failure to find the inward and moral realms of man's being, it cannot find objections to egoistical nihilism. Here one of the crucial documents of our time is the survey of Research into pornography by Maurice Yaffe, published in *The Longford Report*. This was a summary of positivist approaches of a 'scientific' kind which, of course, totally failed to find the problem, which is one of sexual experience, morality and meaning. Yet this approach was applauded by journalists like Bernard Levin and Richard Dixon of *The New Scientist*, who consequently pronounced that there was no harm in cultural debasement. This cold denial of the realities of enslavement and exploitation leaves the way open to Stirnerean nihilism: 'I do not allow myself to be disturbed in my self-enjoyment,' while seeming rational, cool and detached.

By contrast, we have to insist, as Roger Poole insists in his polemic against empiricism, 'some things are *evidently* true or false, good or bad, as when Solzhenitsyn indites the Gulag . . . It is dirtying to one's moral presence in the world to start examining into the meaning of *words* when faced by an appeal like Solzhenitsyn's to one's human responsibilities and feelings in the existentialist life-world.' 'Feeling, subjectivity, has to be respected first . . . if someone tells me about . . . sexual indignities practised on girl students . . . in such a way as to make my heart beat faster . . . then I do not have to examine the meaning of the *words* being used . . . That is not to say, I need not check up on the *evidence* . . . the presence of subjectivity introduces real issues, issues that have to be settled *now*.' (*Empiricism in Crisis*, p. 14). Poole's impatience is with those who cavil in a positivist way about meanings of words, when evident and urgent moral issues are demanding their im-

110

mediate commitment. In their refusal to engage with these existential problems, they leave the way open to nihilism. For nihilism, as we have seen, is the 'refusal to take anything or anyone seriously,' and this marks the new 'amoral' position.

Today, such nihilism is an everyday occurrence. This week (April 1977) in *The Times* a reviewer applauds a novel in which a woman has sex with a bear: a film is discussed in which a man has sex with a pig – in a film displayed with public funds. In *Studio International* it was argued recently that Ian Brady's murders of children could be seen as works of art, because his perception of the Moors in which he buried them must have been altered by his crimes. These are all manifestations of a perverted play which, insofar as we do not reject the implications, involves us in a 'creative Nothingness' that involves us in dissolution. To reject such assaults on human value and freedom is not to resort to the 'police state' or 'censorship': it is to ask whether we should be permitted to exploit human beings like that, and to oblige us to define human value, dignity and freedom once more. Insofar as there is only a craven silence in response to such atrocities, we hear the mocking laughter of Max Stirner.

Chapter Seven

MORE OBSTACLES TO FREEDOM

Once we have grasped the dangers of that kind of nihilism which threatens our way of life, we can see that what happens to consciousness is of major political importance.

Hate is a desperate solution to the *Dasein*-problem, of finding a sense of meaning in the face of nothingness. When culture itself turns to hate and cynicism, then this in turn reinforces the failure of an adequate philosophy. The corruption of art is a serious matter. Susanne Langer says:

> The arts objectify subjective reality, and subjectify outward experience of nature. Art education is the education of feeling, and a society that neglects it gives itself up to formless emotion. Bad art is corruption of feeling. This is a large factor in the irrationalism which dictators and demagogues exploit.
>
> *Philosophical Sketches*, p. 84

We need a philosophy which can come to terms with the human condition as such, and understand its range and variety of modes of understanding. It will not do to leave 'nature' and 'science' as though these were merely to be accepted: they need to be examined as concepts and procedures:

> There can be no resolution of the problem of the *Geistwissenshaften*, Plessner declares, without a general philosophy of man: 'a philosophical anthropology'. But a philosophical anthropology is in turn impossible, he says, unless it is itself founded on a philosophy of nature, not, indeed, in the Kantian sense of a set of principles for the inorganic world, leaving the life sciences to be guided by a vague set of 'as it's' or 'regulative principles', but in the sense of a philosophical question of what it *means to be alive*.
>
> *Approaches to a Philosophical Biology* p. 65.

112

Our groping for solutions must be towards a philosophy, a kind of work in the humanities which is very different from anything we know at present. It is, perhaps, closer to 'English'. F. R. Leavis, in *The Living Principle*, speaks of the training which enables an individual to become creative and to move towards 'spontaneous-creative fullness of being'.

This work is taxing and painful, and this is why education has so often fallen down over its task. Take the present plight of adolescents, who have lost much in the politically-inspired changes in the structure of education. Little or nothing is solved by the administrative changes towards comprehensive education: what was needed was a reform of the content of education, so that, as it became more human, the competitive element was reduced, and all kinds and conditions of children could share the exploration of true human qualities. Here again we have a political danger, in the failure of education to foster processes of personal development which are essential for democracy, while pursuing the chimeras of dogmatic egalitarianism. The real radical changes are those which bring education back to problems of meaning and value, in the search for something to believe. But the adolescent has been captured for commercial exploitation, while the adult is afraid of the pains of self-realization. Meerloo says:

> Becoming conscious of the entity we call ego or self or *I* is a painful mental process. It is not a matter of chance that the feeling of endless longing, of Weltschmerz, is traditionally connected with adolescence. The process of becoming an autonomous and self-growing individual involves separation from the family. To achieve *internal democracy*, the adolescent must separate himself from his protective environment.
>
> *Mental Seduction and Menticide*, p. 297

Meerloo believes our ways of bringing up children in the West may emphasize this problem.

> Whereas primitive groups impose some measure of social responsibility upon the child early in life and increase it gradually, our middle-class culture segregates him completely in the world of childhood, nursery, and schoolroom, and then plunges him precipitately into adulthood to sink or swim. At this turning point, many young people shrink from such a test. Many do not want a freedom that carries with it so many burdens,

113

so much loneliness. They are willing to hand back their freedom in return for continued parental protection or to surrender it to political or economic ideologies which are in fact displaced parental images.

p. 298

We have begun to learn how to contribute to the creative dynamics making for maturity in children at school: the revolution in art teaching has been followed by the creative revolution in English, and now in music.* In many schools children experience a rich exercise of their powers of symbolising, in the pursuit of a sense of meaning in life. But there are also many nihilistic elements gaining ground in schools, while the school-leaver plunges into a cultural desert, to be exploited by 'displaced parental images', and to live among an adult community in which there are few opportunities for 'meeting' and 'confirmation'. This question of how our society treats adolescents is a critical one politically, yet their exploitation is ignored. A Coroner, conducting an inquest on a girl who died at a 'pop' concert said, 'I am not blaming anyone – this is show business.' In some areas adolescents have become virtually ineducable: even among the least exploited one finds a rebellious hostility, inculcated by 'pop', which is spurious.

In this corruption of adolescent life there has been a serious loss of the capacity of the young to contribute to our society. In *Playing and Reality*, D. W. Winnicott discusses the psychological reasons for the adolescent's need for a special kind of 'encounter'. He calls it 'confrontation', which points to a painful but satisfying relationship from which the adult must not flinch. Adults have abrogated their function in this respect, out of fear of painful unpopularity, while deliberate attempts to separate the adolescent from such intercourse with adults, substituting a pseudo-revolt for it, have worsened the situation. The 'pop' world and cinema have thrust on adolescents a spurious, too early sophistication. Under the

* See *Sound and Silence* by John Paynter and Peter Aston, Cambridge, 1970. It must however be said that the creative approach is under assault: see, for example, the neglect of this approach to English in the The Bullock Report, *A Language for Life*. I have attacked this Report in a work entitled *English for Meaning*.

burden of these forms of betrayal and premature responsibility, the young person must 'lose spontaneity and play and carefree creative impulse.' 'One of the most exciting things about adolescent boys and girls', Winnicott says, 'can be said to be their idealism. They have not yet settled down into disillusionment'. If we force too early responsibility on them, this idealism may be lost. 'Responsibility', he says, 'must be taken by parent figures'.

> If parent figures abdicate, then the adolescent must make a jump into a false maturity and lose their greatest asset:freedom to have ideas and to act on impulse.
>
> p. 150

Confrontation must be personal. 'Adults are needed, if adolescents are to have life and liveliness. Confrontation belongs to containment that is non-retaliatory, without vindictiveness, but having its own strength. Let the young alter society, teach grown ups how to see the world afresh: but where there is the challenge of the growing boy or girl, then let the adult meet the challenge. And it will not necessarily be nice . . .' The adult has to face the underlying impulse of the young to *replace* him: 'In the unconscious fantasy these are matters of life and death'. p. 150. Political and social dangers arise from the unwillingness of adults to face the Dasein-problem. Adults do not have sufficient security to endure the unconscious impulse of the adolescents to wish them dead (an impulse which can also provide the adult with much quiet amusement.) The psychotherapist Meerloo, sees the political dangers:

> Alas, the youth's surrender of individuality is no guarantee against fear of loneliness. The real outside world is in no way altered by his inner choice, therefore the youth who relinquishes his freedom to a new parent figures, develops a cautious dual feeling of love and hate towards all authority. . . . The duality is an endless one, for one side of his nature continually seeks to overstep the limits which his other, submissive side has imposed. The man who fails to achieve freedom knows only two enemies: unquestioning submission and implusive rebellion.
> Conversely, the individual who is strong enough to embrace mature adulthood enters into a new kind of freedom . . . an ambiguous concept

115

since it involves the responsibility of making new decisions and confronting new uncertainties. . . .

p. 298

Moreover, the solution itself appears in the light of Meerloo's analysis as a cultural one:

> The inner harmony between social adaptation and self-assertion has to be reformed in every new environment. Each individual has to fight over and over again the same subtle battle that started during infancy and babyhood. The ego, the self, forms itself through confrontation with reality. Compliance battles with originality, dependence with independence, outer discipline with inner morals. No culture can escape this inner human battle . . .

Yet youth is being persuaded that these necessary struggles can be escaped, and this persuasion is combined with the march towards triviality under commercial-industrial pressures. The following observation applies not only to youth, but to us all:

> Radio and television catch the mind directly, leaving children no time for calm, dialectic conversation with their books. The view from the screen doesn't allow for the freedom-arousing mutality of communication and discussion. Conversation is the lost art. These inventions steal time and steal self-awareness. What technology gives with one hand – easiness and physical security – it takes away with the other. *It has taken away affection from relationships between men.* Technical intrusion usurps human relationship as people no longer have to give one another attention and love any more . . . *The impersonal machine replaces human gesture and mutuality* . . .

Our world is reducing creativity and freedom at a disastrous rate. As Meerloo says, 'the world of tomorrow will witness a tremendous battle between technology and psychology . . . It will be a fight of technology versus nature, of systematic conditioning versus creative spontaneity.' This is clearly true as utilitarian influences triumph in education, and commercialism in culture.

Many observers have pointed out the subtle ways in which we come to approach human problems in the 'technological' way. Professor John Macmurray discusses 'the spread of an attitude to life which sees it as a series of problems to be solved, and for which all problems are technological, and what is

116

needed for their solution is a 'scientific' approach un-trammelled by traditional taboos': and this goes with a growing insensitiveness to intrinsic values.

> What is involved can best be seen if we consider out relations to other people. What would it mean if we were to adopt a scientific or technological attitude in this field? We should require to be completely objective, unemotional, impersonal ... we would treat all people as means to our ends or as obstacles to our purses. We should seek to discover how to make use of them, or how to defeat and destroy them. We should in fact looks upon and behave towards other people as if they were things for our use ...
>
> *Religion, Art and Science*, p. 25

Meerloo, as an ex-inmate, can see only too clearly the same nihilism that created the death camps emerging today in our culture and education. The 'optimistic liberal naïveity' of our time adheres also to homunculism. Failing to encounter the problem of existence, it employs its rationalism and its intellectual hate to deny the 'irrational' depths. In the end it comes to deny the creative, formative principle, and man's freedom, by the same paths by which the Weimar Republic led to Nazism. We need to revise our concepts of knowledge, so that we can find and foster what Pestalozzi called the 'whole man'. This requires us to accept the 'irrational' without becoming irrational ourselves: the answer is to be found in the development of those disciplines such as psychoanalysis and phenomenology by which we are learning to study the phenomenon of consciousness. Knowledge obliges us to resist nihilism, and to uphold the 'formative principle' in man, and the reality of his higher nature.

The problem of finding oneself is a philosophical one, and while we are imprisoned in positivism – as manifest in sociology or academic psychology as it is taught today – we can never find ourselves. Yet we remain untroubled, even as students are daily introduced to books, theories and methods which turn people into things, and nullify man.

The newspaper reports of delinquency, mental illness, alcoholism and other forms of distress among youth are seldom connected with this deep philosophical issue. A conference of social workers and doctors in Rheims has focussed

117

attention on the alarming increase of suicides among young French people. In recent years the suicide rate has increased so much among the seventeen to twenty age group that it has become the most important single cause of death. They called for a national campaign against this 'self-destruction' among the young (*Times*, April 28, 1976, p. 6). My analysis of the exploitations of 'pop' and the general tendency of education, culture, and popular attitudes to man reveal the underlying nihilism that prompts such death wishes. The philosophy on which this nihilism is based has been explored and exploded by many, from Husserl to Maslow. Yet how are the young to find the sources which may save them? We need a profound change in education, towards *Humanitas*.

A good deal in our culture and education must convey to students a feeling that everything to do with love must be rejected. Any serious intellectual must dismiss as despicable 'all that is ordinary', as Heidegger and the 'old' existentialism tended to do. All attempts to solve the problem of meaning are doomed.

But under the surface there is much dissatisfaction and yearning, because primary needs are being thwarted. As Leavis has said, 'There is . . . in Humanity an instinct of self-preservation to appeal to – a sense of vital needs thwarted and starved by technologico-Benthamite civilisation'. This revolution requires of us a new 'community of consciousness' – and a new ethical concern with 'human being'. It cannot be done by burning books and destroying data-banks, taking furniture out of the classroom, 'stealing (school) tapes' (once advocated in proposals for radical education). It cannot be achieved by giving over direction and control to students.

Of the 'revolution' now in the air we need to ask, with Marjorie Grene:

> one is likely to ask oneself, as Sartre himself asks of the Communist: what of the revolutionary after the revolution? The philosophy of the free man in its political aspect is the philosophy of transcendence as such, of going beyond the present society to create a new one. At present, in Sartre's picture, it is the dichotomy of oppressor and oppressed that motivates such transcendence. *But what of the free man in the free society?*
> *Introduction to Existentialism*, p. 114 (my italics)

In the Paris rising of 1968, Sartre saw nothing beyond the immediate conflict, and this seems characteristic of many present-day revolts.

In an interview between Sartre and the student leader, Daniel Cohn-Bendit, Sartre said that the student revolutionaries need not worry about a 'programme':

> many people to not understand why you don't try to put forward a programme or try to structure your movement. You are reproached with trying to destroy everything without knowing – or in any case without saying – what you are doing to put in its place . . .

Cohn-Bendit replied that all he sought was:

> to create an *experience* which is a complete break with the society, an experience which will not last but which *will* indicate a possibility. You catch a glimpse of something, and then it's gone. But that at least proves it can exist . . .

> (my italics)

By his confrontation with 'society' the schizoid revolutionary can feel 'real', for a brief episode, in the moment of hate. In such 'acting out' there is a false sense of 'ontological security': one is 'held'. The individual knows it cannot last, and does not hope to find anything beyond the action into which he thrusts his false solution.

Sartre, himself a schizoid individual, feels that this 'false-solution-doing'is 'imagination':

> Your movement is interesting because it puts imagination in power. Your imagination, is, like everybody else's, limited – but you have more ideas than your elders. We have been formed in such a way that we have very precise ideas about what is and what is not possible . . . You have a much richer imagination . . .

All Sartre asks for, however, is something dismally negative – a mere jolt for the bourgeoisie:

> Something which astonishes, something which jolts, something which repudiates all that has made our society what it is today, has come out of your movement. I call it extending the range of possibilities. Don't give up.

> May 20, 1968, *Le Nouvel Observateur*

His 'possibilities' are not human, but possibilities of violent action for its own sake. To him 'violence is man re-creating himself', and freedom is in endless hostility. There is nothing creative beyond his chaos.

Psychoanalysis might see Sartre's attitude to society as a symbolic posture of hate directed at the 'environment' which created him, but did not 'facilitate' his growth to a human identity. Society has to be blamed for being a 'bad parent': the only way to feel real in the absence of a sense of 'being' derived from the parental environment is to attack it, by the ultimate 'false male doing' activity. His 'imagination' has no 'female element' content, no essential creativity, no future. Its effect is limited to 'jolting' and 'astonishing'. It enacts a schizoid protest against 'impingement': an infantile claim that 'they' should 'care', which they do, by wielding truncheons.

Any changes brought about by reform, Sartre believes, will be 'superficial': 'these things will not alter the system fundamentally'. It is impossible to obtain genuine revolutionary 'improvements' in a bourgeois university. The university will remain a 'bourgeois hoax', to him. Sartre is virtually saying that it is not possible to feel human and real in the environment as it is, since 'in my environment I have never managed to feel real'. What is required is some kind of 'anti-environment'.

The deplorable state of French Universities requires immediate reform and justifies strong protest. The linking of universities to commercial and industrial needs must be fought *But I do not feel that Sartre and Cohn-Bendit wanted real change*. All they want is a confrontation, of the 'endless violence' kind which merely satisfies a delinquent need to feel real. The moral intensity of the fanatical nihilist can never discover and allow a point of growth. The naturalism on which their scepticism is based excludes intentionality, because it cannot find man's moral being.

Sartre could never lead a genuine revolution, because he has no sense of the realities of the realm of being. Despite Sartre's struggle in *Being and Nothingness*, he can only find 'being' intellectually. Nowhere in his interview with Cohn-Bendit does Sartre convey any sense of a goal of thought and discipline, no

120

glimpse of human potentialities, no awareness of greater fulfilment of human meaning, towards which a university could strive.

The existentialism of Heidegger and Sartre is a philosophy concerned with the lonely individual, thrown into a threatening world, free to make that world his own, yet never succeeding, falling forever tragically short of the world-creation at which he aims. How can any educational programme be based upon such a philosophy of alienation and despair? The 'old' existentialism as a political force, *must fizzle out*, because it has no future to believe in.

Our philosophical and educational task is to overthrow this approach, because Sartre's world-view is a dead end, contributing to that paralysis which lies behind our present deadness. We may start from a recognition that Binswanger's 'injection' of love into existentialism springs from a belief in love that Sartre could not have.

Our very powers of perception and our successful interaction with the world develop in the context of the mother's 'creative reflection'. The 'introduction of the child into the social world' is made possible by the mother's responsiveness. But there are deeper dynamics, which develop from the mysterious 'meeting' between mother and infant, by which 'between man and man the heavenly bread of self-being is passed' as Buber put it. We live in a mansion of consciousness, which is a product of the reflective 'being for' intersubjectivity of the mother. This consciousness operates through symbolism, which is itself created by *imaginative* processes between mother and infant. The infant discovers the separateness of self and other, and the benign relationship between himself and the world, through his mother's 'creative reflection' of his emerging potentialities, and because she was capable of 'being for' him.

We are able to know the world in ways which are not found among animals because we have been given *culture* by our mothers. The very fact that we are that distinctive *animal symbolicum* is a product of love, for there is no other name for the mother's devoted capacity to be for her child. If our symbols and culture are given us through love, then love is the fundamental principle of the human world.

The observations of psychoanalysis confirm love as the basis of all human capacities. It would be impossible for the infant to develop as an autonomous being with a secure sense of his own identity, without that strange complexity of processes of 'being for', consisting of forms of telepathy, projective identification, imagination and play, which Winnicott associates with the Primary Maternal Preoccupation, and sees as the psychic matrix of our humanness.

Sartre never experienced these, and has had ever since to make himself. Being an intellectual genius, he erects this need into a philosophy which can only deny the possibilities of encounter, since he has never known it. The best account of this blindness is that given by Marjorie Grene in her *Introduction to Existentialism* (originally published as *Dreadful Freedom*).

Marjorie Grene looks critically at Sartre's exposition:

> My relation to another is revealed according to Sartre's example in the moment at which, sitting in a park, I find a stranger looking at me or at least about to look at me.

Earlier, she summarizes Sartre's position thus:

> It is the fact of another's looking at me, Sartre believes, that reveals the existence of another subject – not the mere physical presence of a pair of eyes directed my way but the whole transformation of my world that the look behind those eyes implies. For in that experience of being looked at by another I find myself becoming, not the transcendence I otherwise feel myself to be, but a mere object, a body appearing thus and thus in someone's else's world . . . For the other person, whom I find looking at me, I become *only* a body, a thing within his horizon, as 'objective' as the chair I am setting in.
>
> p. 79

The other existence which thus reveals itself is, at the same time, annihilation of myself as subject: between my freedom and its destruction in another's possession of me, there arises a circle of conflicts. 'Conflict', says Sartre in *L'Etre et le Néant* (p. 431), 'is the original sense of being-for-another'.

In the example of sitting in a park the other person is reading a book: he and the book, like the trees in the park, are objects. If the stranger's eye wanders from his book, over the trees, to me: such a shift in his attention would suddenly reveal me as an *object* in his world. By this possibility the whole world of my consciousness, the whole world as *I* have ordered it, is threatened with disorganization and destruction. The awareness of such a possibility causes, Sartre says, an 'internal haemorrhage' of my world: *it bleeds in the direction of the stranger.*

Sartre's view of the effects of another's gaze upon one is clearly psychopathological: and yet this view has become predominant.

Sartre's is clearly a schizoid view. Experiencing the deep sense of emptiness which R. D. Laing and others have discovered in schizoid patients, he fears implosion and petrification. Like Sylvia Plath, he is obsessed with that blank, stony gaze which menaces one's whole world, that she saw in the moon ('The moon is my mother'). If we accept Winnicott's account of the mirror-role of the mother, we can explain how this dread of what should be the reflection of one's emerging autonomy and freedom can turn into its opposite – a threat of malignant annihilation that can destroy one's whole world. One of Winnicott's infants in *Therapeutic Consultations in Child Psychiatry* ('George') looked into his mother's mind to see her consciousness of himself, *and saw nothing.* Because she did not want him, she obliterated him. *He never recovered.* Something of this kind, I believe, was experienced by Sartre: he experienced this haemorrhage, and feared it in every gaze, erecting it into a philosophy.

Masud Khan maintains that *sexual perversion develops from the protraction into adulthood of primitive attempts to solve these problems when these intersubjective processes go wrong.* The avalanche of perversion in contemporary culture led by Sartre arises from the erection into a philosophy of Sartre's inability to feel any confidence in the love-relationship with the mother, because he never experienced it, and thus tends to substitute hate-relationships. The eroticization of this hostility is pornography.

In *Dreadful Freedom* Marjorie Grene discusses Mathieu's response to his mistress seeing him naked, in *The Age of Reason.* When he is naked with her in love-making, the nakedness is felt to be appropriate. When she, clad, surprises him, naked, and announces her pregnancy, their amatory routine is broken, and he feels himself humiliated. Shame and fear are for Sartre the two proper and immediate reactions to the intrusion of another person into my world. ,

The only alternative to fear and shame if the onlooker threatens me by his looking, is to *turn and look at him*. Thus I in my pride *threaten him with extinction*:

> Hence the principle of conflict – all relations between myself and others are, existentially, a battle to the death. Either he, a person, transcends my transcendence and makes a thing of me, or I in my prouder freedom transcend and so annihilate his liberty.
>
> p. 81

This is a version of the schizoid impulse *to petrify the other before he endangers the empty self.* The satisfaction offered the audience by pornography and other forms of a nihilistic culture is that of annihilating 'the other' (mostly *woman*, since she offered the first such threat as mother) by 'looking at her' – by killing the other, by a malignant gaze. Politically the same futile conflict follows, since everyone other than the proud self is an enemy to one's freedom. But since there can be no 'we' there can be no real politics. The treadmill is, psychotically, endless.

> Even murder cannot change the fact that the victim, by having existed, has threatened and limited my liberty. There can be no knockout blow or even a decision, only round after round of a bout that never stops – and never starts either, for it is a continuous and unbreakable circle.
>
> p. 82

There is no escape from the objectification of myself in a sexual relationship, in Sartre's eyes, except into the bad faith of vanity, which equally destroys me. We cannot escape sexuality, because it is 'ontologically' necessary: nor can we escape from these problems in sex. Love is the wish to be loved.

> Love is the attempt of the Self-seen-as-object to absorb another's freedom by making itself the highest reality, the ground of all significance for that freedom.

Love, thus, to Sartre, carries with it its own frustration, because the beloved turns object in relation to the lover as subject. It is always an attempt to triumph over the other, which is a principle of perversion and pornography.

We can try to love the shame of my object-character, and try to stress and increase it: this is *masochism*, which loves its own frustration. Or I may as subject try to reduce the other to the status of a mere object. This is *indifference*, and is the reduction of the love-object to functional man or woman. But this automaton may well turn its baleful glance on me and objectify me, destroying my illusion or superior solitude.

More aggressively, I may seek to annihilate, rather than ignore, the other's freedom. Desire, for Sartre, is the endeavour to produce the *incarnation* of another subject, to ensnare the other's freedom in the flesh. The achievement of desire lies in the caress, in which the hand makes flesh of the breast or limbs or body of the other, seeming momentarily to transfigure and transcend his freedom. But desire contains its own frustration: pleasure produces a reflective consciousness of itself which becomes an end. As I seek my own pleasure I am distracted from, and lose the aim and awareness of, the other's incarnation.

Here, I cease being flesh and try, using my body, to seize and appropriate the other's liberty.

> So I am a *body* . . . in the face of *flesh* . . . I try to use the object-other to demand of him an account of his transcendence and, just because he is *all* object, he escapes me with *all* his transcendence . . . what I take in my hands is *something else* than what I wanted to take . . . It is this situation which is at the origin of *sadism* . . .
>
> *L'Etre et le Néant*, p. 468

What is strange about Sartre's account of sexuality is that so few have declared, 'This is wrong. This is not how I experience it'. But behind it is Sartre as an infant, desperately trying to find the mother's breasts, her body, and herself, and finding only a desperate menace to himself. Inevitably, that infant summoned the oral, annihilating, appropriating power that lives with the adult schizoid man: a hungry mouth threatening to devour himself and the whole world. *Everything Sartre says about sexuality is mechanical and seen from the outside.*

But, characteristically, our intelligentsia do not notice the bewildered, dissociated, cold-bloodedness, the 'lack of feeling tone' of the severe schizoid. And they turn his hate into a political and cultural programme, itself a *huis clos*. They cannot escape because their basic natural scientism has allowed them to become confounded by the collapse of values and the symbolic system. We are only hopeless in the face of Sartre's persuasions, so long as we fail to be what Husserl calls functionaries of mankind.

The passages Marjorie Grene discusses from *L'Etre et le Néant* read like a prospectus for the cultural degradation of our time:

> What sadism seeks to produce is the obscene, that is, flesh revealed to an observer without desire.
>
> Marjorie Grene, p. 86

But that aim is thwarted, too, since it is the very freedom of the other that the sadist tries to seize, and that freedom constantly escapes him. However, he goes on, as the homosexual Texan murderer, Corll, went on, until he had killed over twenty young men. Or as *Oh! Calcutta!* goes on, as a public act of annihilating others, by exposing their nakedness to the public gaze, and exerting contemputous hostility to human freedom and dignity. Sartre says that

> Sadism discovers that it was *that liberty* it wanted to enslave and realizes the vanity of its efforts. Here we are once more returned from *the-being-who-looks* to the *being-who-is-looked-at*, we do not leave the circle.
>
> *L'Etre*, p. 477

But the circle has become one in which the public, *en masse*, tramps round, endlessly locked in the futility of a culture which seeks to destroy the freedom of others, by debasement after debasement, assault on flesh after assault on flesh – and finds only confirmation of its desperate belief that love and self-transcendence are impossible. Or, to cut a long story short, they are encapsulated in a psychotic inability to feel human or to find 'the heavenly bread of self-being' which is 'passed from one human being to another'.

Not even hate, as a last desperate remedy, can break these bonds. The other *has* been and has been free: that encroachment on my total liberty I cannot cancel or forget. The circle, then, of conflict, on conflict is still unbroken: it is a treadmill from which, in my endeavour to approach another's freedom, I can never escape.

Grene, p. 81

This treadmill has led to the collapse of politics and the futile radicalism manifest in the work of Laing, the Anti-university, and the rest, while the intelligentsia has largely destroyed its own consciousness, in endless hostility of a paranoid-schizoid kind. *It is an encapsulation which can lead us blindly to our doom.*

But Sartre's original example, of the other's gaze in the park, is highly artificial. These two people are abstracted from the personal settings in which they live. As Marjorie Grene says, as soon as two people look at one another in a normal way, 'I project him in imagination into his world, a world of other human beings to whom he stands in an intimate relation, as do I to those whom he, too, can only guess at.' The imaginative act is an entering into the 'mansions of consciousness' in which men may meet, and where we *can* find the other.

We need to invoke that imaginative finding of the other through 'creative reflection' that is possible between mother and infant, which is the infant's first socialization. We all, except severe schizoids, know this finding and meeting, even if we are also aware of the gulfs. We know love *is* possible.

Marjorie Grene rightly invokes that kind of meeting which complies rather than menaces us.

> . . . the sense of *wanting the completion which is just as genuine in human consciousness* as is the ultimate privacy which Sartrean existentialism prefers to stress.
>
> Marjorie Grene. (my italics)

For an account of human beings' need for one another we may turn to Aristophanes in the *Symposium*:

> It is, in other words, some such sense of the original togetherness of particular human beings as that myth conveys that is lacking in Sartre's analysis . . .
>
> *Introduction to Existentialism. p. 88*

It is perverse of existentialism, which boasts that it takes personal growth seriously, to ignore the growth of that unique sense of difference which is the most essential aspect of my nature. Yet consciousness itself, for all its inwardness, evolves out of a pattern of organic relationships from the total dependency of the unborn child on its mother, through the gradual lessening dependence of the infant and young child.

> In that process others are essential to the individual neither as threats to his own liberty nor as mere objects in his world but rather as *the very foundation of that world itself.*

It is significant that a woman philospher should recapture this truth and urge it against Sartre, the truth of *liebende Wirheit*.

As Polanyi points out, Sartre's theories can be seen as part of the development of a 'naturalism' which has had a most destructive effect on the ethical patterns of society:

> The Enlightenment believed that man's moral responsibility would be safely grounded in nature. Rousseau trusted natural man uncorrupted by society: he established the intrinsic rights of great passions, of creative spontaneity and unique individuality. A drier, more mechanistic version of naturalism was developed by Helvetius and Bentham; it reduced man to a bundle of appetites feeding themselves according to a mathematical formula.
>
> Like Rousseau's noble savagery, Freud's libido is restrained by society. But no noble features are ascribed to it: on the contrary, morality is imposed on the libido externally, and this restraint is actually condemned because it produces sickness. Good and evil are replaced by health and sickness.
>
> The parallel movement from Bentham to Marx is determined by the denial of common interests between different social classes. Rightness is no longer achieved then by the triumph of utility over prejudice, but by the triumph of one class over another; good is what contributes to the victory of the proletariat, and evil is the contrary. *Naturalism is thus transformed from a moral command into a doctrine of moral scepticism.*
>
> *Knowing and Being*, p. 43 (my italics)

Alexander Solzhenitsyn sees that what has emerged from such naturalistic modes of thought is the brutal 'realism' that is now a major threat to our human dignity, to our freedom, to 'mutual affection', and to our creative potentialities in the pursuit of meaning.

128

Revolutionary violence and sexual revolution are related by their essential psychopathology, and their historical Sadism:

> The personal immoralist converts his anti-bourgeois project readily into social action by becoming an 'armed bohemian' and thus supporting absolute violence as the only honest mode of political activity. These two lines of antinomianism meet and mingle in French existentialism . . .
>
> *Beyond Nihilism* in *Knowing and Being* p. 17

The present pseudo-revolution is such a Sadist revolution: its anti-bourgeois stance is a brutal and solipsistic assertion of the right to satisfy the pleasure principle – with the psychic entropy of the Death Instinct in the background. Because of this underlying pessimism this highly moral immoralism is now moving increasingly towards a nihilistic fanaticism. It is from this evil path that our intellectual minority need to be diverted – even as they take it, even as they see no way of escape.

A parallel reductionism is at the heart of Marxism, which set out to bring about a society in which man could be truly free and not determined by inimical economic forces. This dichotomy was pointed out by Professor John MacMurray:

> The primary condition of a planned social development and, therefore, of the disappearance of economic determinism in the development of society is the realisation of a society without social classes. And a classless society is a communist society. Communism is, therefore, the necessary basis of real freedom. Marx was perfectly right in describing the new form of society as a human society. For it is the only possible form of social relationship in which human development ceases to be merely an organic process and becomes an activity of rational beings.
>
> *The Philosphy of Communism*, p. 80 Faber, 1933

However, while 'society is persons in relation', the relations between persons are of 'more than one type'. There are the mechanical relationships in which one set of persons uses another set as instruments for their own ends. There are organic relationships in which 'a number of people cooperate for the achievement of a common purpose.'

But MacMurray points to a third kind of relationship

> which consists in the relation of persons as persons, a form of relationship of which friendship is the type.

The peculiarity of these is that they do not 'go through the dialectical processes of social history'. Wherever in the world or in history one looks there is no essential difference in love or friendship between men. 'Such relationships are in their nature eternal, not in the sense that they last for ever, but because they remain essentially the same under any conditions in social life.'

> And they do this because they are the ultimate expressions of what human nature essentially is, quite apart from the particular forms of organization which make up the complex of society under the special conditions of any place or epoch.
>
> p. 66

Such relationships 'cannot be interpreted either in mechanical organic terms, and therefore they constitute the social aspect of that which distinguishes human life from all merely organic life.'

It is this which Marxism denies. The Berlin Wall denies it: the invasion of Czechoslovakia denies it: the way in which betrothed people are sometimes treated in Russia denies it. It is what Solzhenitsyn asserts against a barbarous mentality.

Marxism seeks a society in which man will for the first time be free of economic determinism: yet, since Marxist theory cannot find the realm of 'encounter', and the 'superorganic', it cannot find the existentialist freedom which could be realised and fulfilled by such free social conditions. It cannot find love: and this is why it appeals to Sartre, who left the old existentialism of Heidegger for the loveless politics of Marxism.

What Marxism still lacks is the discovery of human consciousness, and the need for meaning. If these can be demonstrated as a *scientific* discovery, how can scientific Marxism fail to take them into account. Surely only by becoming obscurantist itself? This is the serious political danger of Marxism. We have seen that science, applied to human affairs, can be menacing because it cannot 'find' essential human qualities. While Marxism bases itself on this positivist 'science', it also preserves its basis by absolute power, so that neither 'science' nor its application may be criticised or altered. It is this fundamental absurdity of its 'dialectical' materialism that generates the atrocities delineated by

Solzhenitsyn, demonstrating again the importance of what happens in the human consciousness. It is *there* that the death-camps are built, and the collective forms of psychopathology are generated, even in the depths of the 'shadow', when the subjective, and the interaction of subjectivities, are denied or ignored.

Here it may be relevant to add a note on the growing influence of the Sociology of Education, a discipline dominated by 'objectivity' and influenced by materialistic Marxism. Professor Basil Bernstein has urged attention to the ideological assumptions behind the curriculum, teaching and forms of assessment. From his point of view, knowledge is not neutral and disinterested but is 'inextricably linked to the interests of those who produce it.' Marxists believe that traditional liberal educational philosophy produces and validates existing values and practices in education. They would replace it with a 'social' view of knowledge. On the Left this is interpreted to mean that teachers should not formally teach anything but rather assist children to 'make their own sense of the world' except, of course, for a little help from Marxist dogma.

Thus, knowledge is not the product of a few great men, whose achievement we respect. Children are supposed presumably to creat science and art, *ab ovo*, for themselves. This, of course, is to fail to see that, from the beginning, culture and learning are processes that depend upon a complex interaction between tradition, encounter, and the internal dynamics of the person. We only create through interaction with others, and by taking the culture of our civilisation into ourselves, as an instrument of our spontaneity.

To reject 'psychology' is to reject consciousness, and all that subjective disciplines have discovered about it in the last century. It is characteristic of Marxism, as an 'objective' discipline, that it should discard everything that people such as Freud, Jung, Melanie Klein, Winnicott, and others have found out about psychic realities. The growth of the human identity in psychic parturition is hardly a matter of 'class' or 'interests', though these affect the 'condition' in which it takes place

131

All knowledge, sociologists of the 'objective' kind declare, is socially caused and derived. Only gain control of 'society' and you can control knowledge. In *Knowledge and Control*, edited by Michael Young, Bernstein suggested that his ideas would stand a better chance in a society in which there were strong constraints upon the development of a wide range of ideologies. We can detect in this an irritation that life and knowledge – and *human beings* – are so intractable, while in the title of the book lurks the 'objective' impulse to control life, out of a schizoid fear of it, and out of a fear of freedom. Bernstein yearns, according to Tom Cross(*The Times*, August 5th 1974), for a situation in which 'the educational system was a major agency of political socialization'. This impulse is as deadly, as nihilistic, as Behaviourism, or fanatical immoralism, surely?

Michael Young, in *The Educational Review*, says that 'if all knowledge is a social and historical product, then we have no grounds for discovering the worth, truth, or value of anything.' Thus the sociology of education comes to be nihilistic, recognising neither the inward 'ethical sense' of the individual who seeks his authenticity, nor the construction of values by encounter and collocation between men. Tom Cross calls Bernstein's view a 'persuasive absolutism', since Bernstein means that knowledge may be used by his kind of educational system, not to pursue and spread the truths of existence, but to serve a political end. His politics of education thus serves the same controlling impulse as those which impel Pavlov, or B. F. Skinner. Such an approach is coercive and authoritarian.

Tom Cross asks whether the inexperience of the student and the young teacher should be exposed to a superficially compelling hypothesis which has always led in practice to a restrictive form of society where open enquiry is denied by its own suppositions. Cross believes that this movement is altering the whole perspective of teacher training, and he suggests that a strong public debate is necessary where at the moment there is none.

Education in a democracy, its imperfections notwithstanding, must remain an open door into a world where contrary opinions are tolerated as an insurance against dogmatism on any side. To argue an exclusive social view of knowledge, without any clear definition in advance of what that would be, is to seek to close and bolt that door.

The Times, August 5th, 1974

Sociology has hardly yet entered upon its own crisis, though this is coming, with the recognition of subjective realities. But in the meantime, its objectivity, with its implicit nullification of man, impels it towards Marxism and 'scientific' politics, with a large dose of dogmatism and coercion inherent in the ignorant dynamic of the new sceptical fanaticism. I call it ignorant, because no-one who had every *experienced insight* could talk as Bernstein and Young do. No-one who had studied the nature of knowing in *The Knower and the Known* would support attempts to introduce 'strong and effective restraints' upon the emergence of other ideologies, since this is to restrain thought. No-one who has ever really *known* anything could speak, like Michael Young, of how 'we have no grounds' for ethical choice, or as if we had no sense of authenticity within us. If we have 'no grounds for deciding the worth, truth, or value of anything', why is a Marxist solution better than any other? Just as Sartre shows that he prefers, by his moral code, Resistance heroes to fascist ones, so must Michael Young prefer Marxist tenets to bourgeois ones: so he cannot really mean what he says. What he does mean is that values, truth and worth are manifestations of a 'bourgeois hoax', which disguises class interests as liberal meanings. The intense activity of this 'sociology of education' makes it clear that behind its objectivity lurks a fanatical immoralism that would leave many young people without a sense of values and meaning, and with only nihilism or Marxism as alternatives.

In a wider sense, as Rom Harré has pointed out*, attempts to improve the quality of life by altering the tidal flow of the 'system' are doomed to failure, since they leave the 'fine grain of human life' untouched. It is in the fine grain that 'the ritual practices are seated by which respect and contempt for persons is generated'.

I have tried to show that love is a fundamental ground of our existence, and must be recognised in politics and educa-

---

* *Times Higher Educational Supplement*, 9 April, 1976, p. 15.

tion. This was recognised by a scientific symposium conducted at the Massachussets Institute of Technology in 1958, under the leadership of Abraham Maslow. I discuss this seminar in my final chapter. But what happened between 1958 and the seventies? In the House of Lords, in January 1975, the Government was challenged over sex education, and told that it was infringing the Declaration of Human Rights, which recognised the family as the basic unit of society. The government was giving money to organizations which, like the FPA, both made money out of contraceptives, and disseminated propaganda which attacked *love*, by such slogans as 'If you have it off, have it on'. When Lady Elles asked Lord Crowther-Hunt, for the government, that children should be encouraged to explore the moral issues, and be taught to distinguish right from wrong, she was accused of wanting a totalitarian society. Yet, as we have seen, the essence of the creation of a totalitarian society was its deliberate destruction of values in a nihilistic way. It was in Nazi Germany that young girls were for the first time exposed to propaganda for promiscuity. It is in democracy that we assume, in the background, moral health based on love and the family.

What has happened, since the turn of the mid-century, so that intelligent people can declare that they are uncertain about values, and dare not speak of love? What has happened, that they are willing to connive at the destruction of those human qualities on which democracy depends?

The answer to the loss of confidence in our culture and the decline into the inversions of hate, is to embrace those psychologies and philosophies which encounter love. In education we must care for the utterances of our students, and try to understand them, while accepting the inevitable 'confrontation'. Whenever one argues in favour of the dynamics of love, one meets the fear and hostility of the more-or-less schizoid individual in the university and other institutes of higher education. Fortunately we need no longer rely upon a commonsense emphasis on love and 'meeting' between ourselves and our students, which your cold and defensive type can reject with a sneer. There is now enough sound work in phenomenology, philosophical biology, and philosophical anthropology to equip us with formidable arguments, with essentially *rational* arguments, based on many years of work with mental patients, people in ordinary difficulties, and children. They way beyond nihilism and all the degradations and evils to which it has led is in the vindication of the dynamics of love and creativity, in the study of man as animal symbolicum and his need for meaning, in the face of death and nothingness: the *Dasein* problem.

Chapter Eight

NEW BEARINGS BEYOND NIHILISM

Marion Milner writes of her own drawings:

> The drawings were intuitive rather than logical reflections about living, they were attempts to express the wholeness of certain attitudes and experiences which logic and science, by their very nature, can never do; since logic is bound to abstract from whole experience and eliminate *the totality of the particular and the personal.*
>
> *On Not Being Able to Paint*, p. 123

She goes on to distinguish between intellectual and intuitive knowledge, and then to emphasise *the value of the disciplines of creativity.* There remains much more to explore of the nature of these 'other' forms of knowledge based on intuition and imagination.

If civilisation is ebbing, it is ebbing first in men's thoughts. The first problem is to turn back the tide there. The paralysis which is overtaking us is a paralysis of intentionality. As Teilhard de Chardin has said, 'It is too easy to find excuses for inaction by pleading the decadence of civilisation, or even the imminent end of the world. This defeatism, whether it be innate or acquired or a mere affectation, seems to me the besetting temptation of our time. Defeatism is invariably unhealthy and impotent; can we also prove it is unjustified? I think so.'

To escape from this spiritual paralysis requires that we should find again 'the category of life', and, with this, the reality of man's moral being.

The empirical disciplines have not provided what was sought. Students take up such disciplines in the university in the hope of finding the essence of being human.

136

The principle aim of all these theories was to prove the unity and homogeneity of human nature. But if we examine the explanations which these theories were designed to give, the unity of human nature appears extremely doubtful.

Cassirer, *An Essay on Man*, p. 21

Each philosopher or scientist imagines he has found the mainspring. But their theories contradicted one another. They were determined empiricists: 'they would show us the facts and nothing but the facts.' But their interpretations contained arbitrary assumptions:

Nietzsche proclaims the will to power; Freud signalises the sexual instinct; Marx enthrones the economic instinct. Each theory becomes a procrustean bed on which the empirical facts are stretched to fit a preconceived pattern.

p. 21

Our theory of man has thus lost its intellectual centre, and there has grown instead an anarchy of thought. To combine all the aspects of man explored by the various disciplines has become impossible, so each author merely offers us a personal theory. We no longer possess any clear idea of man:

No former age was ever in such a favourable position with regard to the sources of our knowledge of human nature. Psychology, ethnology, anthropology and history have amassed an astoundingly rich and constantly increasing body of facts. Our technical instruments for observation and experimentation have been immensely improved, and our analyses have become sharper and more penetrating. We appear, nevertheless, not yet to have found a method for the mastery and organization of this material. When compared with our own abundance the past may seem very poor. But our own wealth of facts is not necessarily a wealth of thoughts. Unless we succeed in finding a clue of Ariadne to lead us out of this labyrinth, we can have no real insight into the general character of human culture; we shall remain lost in a mass of disconnected and distintegrated data which seems to lack all conceptual unity.

An Essay on Man, p. 22

This 'mass of data' in all its disintegrative effect is now being conveyed to children and youth, during their education, in such a way as the menace values, and their sense of 'what it is to be human'*.

In finding man to be the *animal symbolicum*, Cassirer has opened the door to solutions. Significantly, he discusses the work of the biologist Johannes von Uexküll, whose view of man puts culture and symbolism at the centre. Uexküll's science does not dismiss this central reality of our existence as something 'merely subjective', or so vague that science cannot take account of it.

> Every organism is, so to speak, a monadic being. It has a world of its own because it has an *experience* ot its own . . . The *experiences* – and therefore the *realities* – of two different organisms are incomensurable with one another. In the world of the fly, says Uexküll, we find only 'fly things': in the world of a sea urchin we find only 'sea urchin things' . . .
>
> p. 23 (my italics)

When we turn to man, 'man things' belong to a 'symbolic system'. Man rewrites the biological processes in a new dimension:

> This new acquisition (the symbolic system) transforms the whole of human life. As compared with the other animals man lives not merely in a broader reality; he lives, so to speak, in a new *dimension* of reality . . .
>
> p. 24

Once we have recognised this we are on the way to solving our problem: for this reality, not least from the position of the philosphical biologist, thrusts upon us not only truths about ourselves, but certain responsibilities and creative obligations which we have because of our essential nature.

Even the definition of man as the *animal rationale* was too great a limitation:

> instead of defining man as *animal rationale* we should define him as *animal symbolicum*. By so doing we can designate his specific difference and we can understand the new way open to man – the way of civilisation
>
> p. 26

Seeing, *sensing* and *learning* are not *seen* by many theoreticians, some of whom predominate in spheres such as the training of

---

* A sociologist at the University of Sussex, concerned with education, told me it takes a whole year for students trained in Sociology to 'find' the reality of fantasy.

teachers. As Erwin Straus says, 'Fascinated by the object, we are, in everyday life, inclined to forget the seeing because of the visible'. With 'seeing', knowing and learning are often forgotten, too. Marjorie Grene points out that the question of how we know, raised in a dialogue of Plato's, has never been answered by philosophy. She is close to Polanyi in asserting that 'there is never anything else other than persons knowing'.

The Humanities teacher and the literary man often turn to philosophy hoping to find an account of 'What it means to be, both in perception *and* motility, in serving *and* performing, "an experience being"?' Too often, what he gets is either a frank rejection of the possibility of such an account, or the avoidance of all such questions.

As Husserl says,

> The genuine spiritual struggles of European humanity as such take the form of struggles between the philosophies, that is, between the sceptical philosophies – or non-philosophies, which retain the word and not the task – and the actual and still vital philosophies. But the vitality of the latter consists in the fact that they are still struggling for their own true and genuine humanity. To bring latent reason to the understanding of its own possibilities and thus to bring to insight the possibility of metaphysics as a true possibility – this is the only way to put metaphysics or universal philosophy on the strenuous road to realization.
>
> Crisis, p. 15

This is the only way to decide whether the *telos* inborn in European humanity at the birth of Greek philosophy is merely a delusion, or whether Greek humanity was not rather the first breakthrough to what is essential to humanity as such, its *entelechy*.

> To be human at all is essentially to be a human being in a socially and generatively united civilization: and if man is a rational being (*animal rationale*), it is only insofar as his whole civilization is a rational civilization, that is, one with a latent orientation toward reason or one openly orientated toward the entelechy which has come of itself, and which now of necessity consciously directs human becoming. Philosophy and science would accordingly be the historical movement through which universal reason, 'inborn' in humanity as such, is revealed.
>
> pp. 15–16

The dominant philosophy today clearly does not belong to

this movement. Its basis of criticism is formal logic, and students are not meant to know – or possess – what the great men of the past have said about human existence. They are to learn to assess the logic of their arguments by a procedure which is to philosophy as mathematics is to physics. They are to have no respect for philosophical achievements, not even those of Plato and Aristotle, and they are never to *believe* anything. Any idea that they are concerned with the 'meaning of a genuine humanity' must be dismissed.

It does not matter *who* puts forward any appealing philosophical argument: the student is to be trained in the clever impertinence of picking holes in it. No wonder English specialists like Leavis declare themselves anti-philosopher! What they should declare is that they are 'anti-non-philosopher', since the fashionable training is in philosophical destructiveness, that is, in the trivillisation of philosophy, and the avoidance of all problems. The area of the process of knowing, its tacit core, as defined by Polanyi from a lifetime of rational scientific research, will be excluded from the philosopher's scope. It is interesting to speculate how such a philosopher can confidently examine religion, while the truths of experience as explored by poetry or music would seem to be beyond his scope, since most of these truths are 'inward'. The values bound up with knowing, or the truths of experience revealed by psycho-analysis would also be beyond the scope of philosophy, as currently defined. We only have to think of the complex logic of a creative work, like *King Lear* or Mahler's *Ninth Symphony*, to see that philosophy, as practised today, must necessarily be an enemy to the quest for truth. Their logic is totally different from formal logic: but logic it is, as we have seen in looking at the dynamics of love and hate. The truths of the world are left by philosophy to 'natural science'. Where, between positivist examinations in the logical mode of facts ascertainable to analytical 'philosophy', and the em-piricism of the natural scientist, are we to place the quest which Husserl urges upon us as the proper duty of philosophy? The whole 'continental' tradition is scrupulously ignored, while the student can get a degree in 'Philosophy' without ever having had a philosophical experience.

Such philosophy is simply a training in problem-dodging. It must avoid any recognition that philosophical problems really exist, and must be answered. Many philosophers simply declare the asking futile: 'We can also bark at the moon' says A. L. Melden in *Free Action*. Yet, as the struggles of the great artists show, the human soul refuses to cease to ask philosophical questions.

It is therefore encouraging to find philosophers like Professor Grene who write of the need to explore the Kantian question, 'What is man?'

> Not only do some of us, however – driven by the motives to speculation which Kant has told us are inescapable, though hopeless, drives of the human mind – want to bark at the moon. We believe that, in view of the conceptual and moral inadequacies of the still powerful alternative behaviourist position, we ought to undertake this (to empiricists) seemingly fruitless task: that we ought to seek, in fundamental reflection, to renew speculative daring and to justify the fundamental belief about man and nature which, outside the psychological laboratory – and, as Straus demonstrates even inside it – we still, and irresistably, hold. We believe, in short, in line with Burtt's critique of Strawson, that metaphysics should set itself not only a descriptive, but a revisionary task.
>
> *Approaches to a Philosophical Biology.* p. 186

Most of us have had a glimpse of the conceptual inadequacies of the behaviourist position, because we can see that a rat in one of their cages is subjected to a simplicity of experimentation which is superficial and 'owes its sham existence to a scotoma for the actual problems', while the theory behind it is 'not objective but totally permeated by unexamined metaphysical and epistemological assumptions.' *

As Cassirer says, 'it is only in our immediate intercourse with human beings that we have insight into the character of man.'

> We cannot discover the nature of man in the same way that we can detect the nature of physical things. Physical things may be described in terms of their objective properties, but man may be defined only in terms of his consciousness. Empirical observations and logical analysis . . . here proved inefficient and inadequate.
>
> *An Essay on Man*

* Erwin Straus, *The Primary World of Senses.*

We must reject the behaviourists and cybernetics experts, because they want to believe that we are no more than a machine. Some leave us no alternative between 'material' existence and 'non-materialism':

> If we accept the proposition that the brain *is* a machine, then in principle – if not in practice – we can build a machine like it. But if we wish to insist that the creative brain is not a machine – that it operates in a vitalistic, non-materialistic basis, not definable in mechanistic terms, then we cannot hope to build a machine like it.
>
> Grene, *Approaches.*

This is the predicament of those imprisoned in Cartesian dualism. If we accept that there is nothing but a 'materialistic' basis for mind, then we should be able to build one, once we know the 'laws':

> Newell, Shaw and Simon are explicit in their conviction that free human behaviour is based on a complex but determinate set of laws. In their view, if we are to produce, mechanically, creations of human quality, we must discover these laws, and we must devise a machine and a program complex enough to embody them and their implications.
>
> *Computers and the Human Mind,* Donald G. Fink, p. 275

Fink and those he quotes are talking of something dead. Marjorie Grene helps make our doubts more articulate:

> First the concepts of cybernetics are unable to take account of the temporal structure of actions. Actions are directed to achievements; and so are machines. Hence the plausibility of cybernetical models. But in fact the principles of cybernetics, like those of classical behaviourism, once more reduce actions of mechanistically conceived and causal chains in a monolithic time series. Organic time, however, is structured in reference to natural goals . . .
>
> Grene *Approaches*, p. 138

That is, a computer cannot initiate, cannot sustain itself, cannot decide to climb a hill, or begin to question the point of its existence. It can only be made on the principles of mechanistically conceived causal chains, which *a man* initiates and directs towards answers which *a man* asks the computer to solve for him. It is neither 'vitalism' nor 'non-materialistic' to point to the fact that it is only living creatures which belong to the organic structure of time, which think – they think, not their brains – and which initiate questions and *learn*:

> the 'learning' of learning machines is only a pseudo-learning: a machine that plays a game, for instance, is programmed to avoid the wrong moves. But a person who learns to play a game stores up information in such a way as *to be able* to make, flexibly, a variety of moves. Machine-learning eliminates potentialities, but does not, as true learning does, create them . . . Machines always work in a complete yes-no fashion. There is always a pair of alternatives, one of which is avoided. But living things display . . . 'anti-logic': so that they respond to situations in self-qualifying ways with a 'yes-and-no' of which no machine – at least no digital computer – is capable . . . They can do this because their relations to their environments, their way of being in and over against it, always involves, as long as they are alive, openness and restriction at one and the same time.
>
> Marjorie Grene, *Approaches* p. 138

To talk, with Edward de Bono, of *The Mechanics of Mind* is to talk nihilistic absurdities, because nothing is or can be known to link the physiological processes with knowing. Such implications are always reductive of man himself. Of course, computers are valuable and may be seen as amazing products of man's intelligence. But it seems characteristic of the excitements and impulses of science and technology that instead of developing a deeper sense of man's mystery, potentialities and dignity, some scientists become reductive and arrogant, and want to deny the category of life in all its complexity and mystery.

The menace of reductionism arises from conceptual, epistemological and methodological confusions in science itself.

> C. F. A. Pantin has recently pointed out, not only the biological sciences but geology, too, must rely for its operation on much broader and more varied contacts with our ordinary environment than mathematical physics permits itself. Pantin calls all these 'unrestricted' sciences, as distinct from the restricted science, of which physics is typical.
>
> *Approaches*, p. 119

Thus, what is happening is an extension of the range and scope of science: 'no one can seriously deny the impressive body of knowledge accumulated by these less restricted techniques or forbid their inclusions among the established sciences.' Psychoanalysis, semiology, phenomenology, and even literary criticism must be allowed into the rational study of life – and, if that is how 'science' is to be defined, into science. But, in a parallel area, philosophical anthropology needs to be developed as a central Humanities discipline.

To see that some philosophers are demanding this extension of science will enable us to resist those powerful impulses often found in science to explain man away. Science often reveals an impulse to exert its will on our inward life, in the attempt to control what must not be controlled if we are to preserve our creativity. Pavlov's ambition was quite clear:

> Pavlov puts his trust in the possibility of subjecting psychic life to 'engineering' by means of objective research. 'Guided by the similarity or identity of various kinds of manifestations, science will sooner or later apply the accrued results of objective research to our subjective world and will thus, quite suddenly, brightly illuminate our nature which is now veiled by darkness. It will illuminate the mechanism and life-value of that which most concerns and binds man, the mechanism of his spiritual life and 'torments'.'
>
> *The Primary World of Senses* p. 39

This tradition has a historical basis which is worth examining from the point of view of the humanities.

> At the Nixon Symposium of 1968, a conference of a small number of outstanding psychologists, physiologists, and psychiatrists, Lashley (as speaker for this group) formulated an 'article of common faith' upon which, he thought, all the participants could agree. This 'article states that all phenomena of behaviour and of mind will ultimately become describable in terms of the mathematical and physical sciences.'
>
> Straus: *The Primary World of Senses* p. 106

As Straus points out, Descartes would have been no stranger at such a meeting, which shows that the 'Cartesian division of the body and soul still continues and keeps even those under its spell who reject it.'

> For what is contested is the very fact that there exists consciousness as an autonomous essence, as a kind of substance which can affect bodily processes.

144

Descartes advanced the same postulate as Lashley centuries ago, though he had limited it to animal behaviour and the human body. 'By adding "and of mind" to the words "of behaviour" the conference had modified and radicalized his opinion on a decisive point.'

> And like a clock composed of wheels and counter-weights . . . the body of a man behaves, being a sort of machine so built up and composed of nerves, muscles, veins, blood and skin, that it would not cease to have the same motions . . .
>
> Descartes, *Meditations*, VI, 33

Philosophical anthropology is anti-Cartesian: trying to put the mind back into the body, the ghost back into the machine, to restore unity out of dualism.

This is of more than mere philosophical-academic interest, for many moral disasters have come from the effects of Cartesian dualism. Linked with the 'objectivity' of Galilean and Newtonian science, it has meant that our approach to man is full of nihilism and deadness. For instance, as Straus says of behaviourism:

> The relation of the subject to sensing is mere 'having'. The subject *has* sensations, but he does not sense. It is a strange world of the dead that is supposed to be the beginning of the foundation of psychic life.
>
> p. 19

In many areas of modern thought attempts are being made to bring the subject to life: to emphasise *sentio ergo sum* rather than *cogito ergo sum*; to emphasise *sensing*, and to rediscover consciousness as an autonomous essence at one with the fabric of the body.

Behaviourism has its own idealism. Pavlov's ambition was to use science to light up the dark areas of 'undefined obscure powers dwelling within (the intellect's) own boundaries' because these 'can only lead . . . into unforeseen material losses and unspeakable suffering in wars and revolutions with all the accompanying terrors that breed bestiality and brutality among man. Only the younger science, only it, shall rescue man from the prevailing darkness and the present outrage in the sphere of interhuman relations.'

145

But such an impulse to save man by conditioned reflexes (says Straus) is likely to lead to ever worse brutality,

> namely by that of mechanical training that would destroy humanity altogether, together with freedom and moral responsibility. Let us hope therefore, that we are spared these wonders of training . . .

But 'objective' psychology has a plan which suits a technological eye:

> Man can become happy by mechanisation only because he himself is nothing but a complex structure of mechanisms: so says Pavlov . . .

This way of thinking is found outside the psychological laboratory, as we have seen, and it lies behind the homunculism and nihilism of our ethos.

A person differs from an animal in being able to question the meaning of his existence. Because of this preoccupation with meaning, man is driven from infancy to develop his creativity, to employ on his existential problems his capacity for symbolism as his 'primary need'. If we do not see this, we do not see man. But the danger is that our reality *becomes* an objectified reality, and our primary life has become tyrannised over by 'modern objective thought'. One of our aims must be the restoration of the 'primary life world' with which the artist and poet have always been concerned.

As Marjorie Grene says:

> As human beings we dwell primarily, and immediately, in the life world; as participants in modern Western culture we acquire, as we mature, the intellectual framework of modern objective thought, within that primary frame. But – and this is the point in our present context – as we acquire our cultural heritage, we come to dwell in it also. We assimilate it to our persons and identify it on the one hand with our primary world and on the other with reality itself. So nature comes to *mean* to us Galilean nature, and the existence of the primary life world is ignored.
>
> pp. 12–13

This separation from nature and from a community in touch with nature adds both to the individual's problem of finding a meaning in existence, and also to his capacity to *live out* a denial of the primary life-world in his very modes of existing. In this originate many of the forms of malaise in our time: we conceive of ourselves *as* the creatures of 'objectivity', in whom there is no place for primary needs. Yet we cannot find our freedom unless we recognise these needs.

But the answer is no Luddite one. The crisis is an inevitable consequence of what Marjorie Grene calls the 'trilemma' of the 'Cartesian-Humean-Behaviourist' position. We have to extract ourselves painfully and slowly, so that:

> freed of an untenable dualism or an absurd reductivism, we (can) stand at last, within the animal kingdom yet other than it, on firm and even ground . . .
>
> *Approaches*, p. 103

We must strive towards a completely new philosophy of Nature. We must make our way step by step through the confusions which arise from the fact that in so many spheres the account of man has left out his creativity, his existence in the body, and the way in which he belongs to the natural world. These aspects of man's being are being painfully restored to our thinking. The Humanities teacher must try to understand the underlying philosophical problems of biology.

For instance, it is not an inevitable implication of science that things simply 'are'. There is no cause in science to deny 'levels', values or meanings.

It is not true that things only '*are* or *are not*', though this is what every child is virtually taught by his science training in school. It is absurd that a child looking at an amoeba through a microscope should be taught that there are no 'levels of being', since the amoeba is incapable of looking at him in the same way: yet it has a self-directedness which the water it exists in has not. Where reality is reduced to 'that which can be measured', and thus to mathematical relationships, there is often an implicit denial of the reality of the consciousness that employs the tools of science

It is not that there is a split between 'two cultures' or a 'dissociation of sensibility'. Modes of thought based on fallacious extrapolations of scientific methodologies and assumptions are destroying recognition of the creative dimension to which science itself belongs. As Marjorie Grene says, discussing Adolf Portmann:

Each of us lives ... in a primary life world, and of which and within which the world of science, or of any other highly articulate discipline develops. Portmann has repeatedly emphasised the importance of giving due heed to *both* these aspects of our lives. By the world of primary experience he means, however, something more inclusive than the concept of the 'life world' ... may suggest. The world in which, from infancy, we come to live, and the human world shared by members of all cultures, does, of course, include the surface of experience, the colours, the sounds, the rhythms of movement that confront us on all sides. But it includes also our feelings, our desires, our dreams, the creative aspiration of artists, the vision of saints and prophets, even the delusions of the insane. No single term can adequately characterise this whole range of primary experience; perhaps we can remember that it is more than the plain, open order of 'common sense' to which we are referring. Such life world, then, with all its opacities and ambiguities, stands in contrast with the limited but lucid sphere governed by operations of the intellect – and that means, in our culture, by the operations of science and technology. Human culture comprises both and can dispense with neither.

Approaches, p. 50

It is this life-world 'with all its opacities and ambiguities' to which post-Kantian philosophy, psychoanalysis, philosophical biology (Goldstein, Portmann, Plessner) and philosophical anthropology are concerned to draw attention. Here the philosophy of science is itself rediscovering the poetic, even as the Arts lose confidence in the imagination. Marjorie Grene goes on:

It has been truly said, 'In a world in which the apparatus of gleaming glass, the bright research laboratories, and men and women in white have acquired an almost symbolic value, we must look again and see how great is the darkness out of which the intellect wells up,' We must try, in other words, to achieve anew a whole vision of our nature – a revision which by its very character research alone is unable to provide.

ibid, p. 51

Academic psychology has contrived a careful perspective whereby it excludes from its discourse all those tacit, imaginative forms of 'subception' or 'indwelling' by the exercise of which the disciplines of psychology can themselves exist. It excludes the man who sees, senses and knows. This psychology has exiled the poetic from its scope and thus the whole roots of our being. By so doing it has influenced the teachers who have trained our youth to think of themselves in

148

the 'perspectives of modern objectivism', to think of themselves as essentially not human, and that transcendence that makes life worth living as unattainable.

Also inculcated by 'objectivism' is a fundamental irresponsibility, a refusal of creative and ethical commitment to the world. The 'I' who is looking at the amoeba, with all the capacities to perceive and give meaning to a world, is left out. Such seeing and sensing are not *seen*, together with their rich apprehension of modes of being in time. Reality is felt to be non-human, totally objectified, like the passive subjects of empirical experiment. It is not a reality which we have created by seeing. The world is not the one we *make*, by intentionality, by the shaft of attention we direct at it.

Thus, the homunculus offered us by psychology, sociology, sexology, by natural scientism, is one for which we feel no responsibility. This explains the strange lack of protest in our world, as dehumanisation overtakes us. The homunculus belongs to the world of the I-It, and we do not encounter him through the I-Thou.

Recovery cannot be merely intellectual, but the first problem is that of seeing the problem itself. This is the first task of 'philosophical anthropology': philosophical examination of the question of what it means to be alive.

Culture and civilisation are, it is commonly assumed, imposed as a veneer on an unwilling animal structure, as in traditional Freudianism. But Marjorie Grene insists, from scientific evidence, that even in the development of the embryo, 'we are biologically formed to be cultural animals'.

> the whole structure of the embryo, the whole rhythm of its growth, is directed, from first to last, to the emergence of a culture-dwelling animal – an animal not bound within a predetermined ecological niche like the tern or the stag or the dragonfly or even the chimpanzee, but, in its very tissues and organs and aptitudes, born to be *open to its world*, to be able to accept responsibility, to make its own the traditions of a historical past, and to remake them into an unforeseeable future.
>
> p. 48

As Bernard Towers and John Lewis have said*, many

* See *Naked Ape – or Homo Sapiens?* Garnstone Press 1964

students have been driven away from science because of the implicit pessimism in its reductionism, and because of the way in which it seemed to reduce man's stature, his responsibility, and his creativity. Many teachers in the Humanities feel the same, and they know that such views menace the values with which they are concerned. Yet they find the same reductiveness confirmed by many in the so-called 'creative' world.

In the work of Marjorie Grene, and those scientist-philosophers she examines, it becomes clear that to fly from science for such reasons is based on a misunderstanding of science. Those scientists who can find the 'whole life world' show themselves capable of finding in the natural world itself manifestations of creativity which illuminate the special level of being which man represents, and the very special creativity which is his. There is more hope in the new biology that is discovering culture as a primary human fact than there is in the world of the Arts today.

What chance is there of our becoming, as Husserl urges us to become, 'In our philosophy, then, – how can we avoid it? . . . *functionaries of mankind.*' ?

What is quite clear, wherever we look, is that whoever it may be, it is no longer the artist who accepts the role of 'functionary of mankind'. Nor is Husserl's burden, to seek means by which we may become able to believe, taken up by the intellectual today, not even in education or the Humanities. The political implications are serious, because democracy depends upon maturity which can tolerate responsibility. But those who belong to the intellectual minority have opted for irresponsibility, for infantile regression, or immaturity: for what *The Guardian* calls 'the new amoral society we have created'. To understand the abysmal nature of the betrayal, we need to return to the fifties, to pick up painfully, if we can, the radical determination manifest in humanistic psychology, which has suffered such setbacks in the period since, but which once pointed in a quite different new direction.

Chapter Nine

CONCLUSIONS

New Knowledge in Human Values and our Betrayal to the Atomic Fire

I wish to end by giving an account of a symposium led by Abraham Maslow, held in 1957, from which some papers were published in 1959: *New Knowledge in Human Values*. Not only does it indicate how catastrophic has been the intellectual betrayal in the Humanities: it also suggests what work we still have to do, or rather, where we have to *begin*. Maslow's point was that it now appears possible for man, by his own philosophical and scientific efforts, to move towards self-improvement and social improvement. (p. viii). This new approach was not to be based on traditional beliefs, all of which, Maslow declares, 'have proved to be failures (our present state proves this to be so).' There *was* a cure for our present disease: 'We need a validated, usable system of human values, values that we can believe in and devote ourselves to because they are true rather than because we are *exhorted* to 'believe and have faith'. (p. viii). Here, then, was the indication of a possible humanistic way of believing, which did not depend upon exhortation, authority, or traditional Christian beliefs, but on the recognition of realities within man's own make-up, and of his existential freedom.

> This volume springs from the belief, first that the ultimate disease of our time is valuelessness; second *that this state is more crucially dangerous than ever before in history*; and, finally, that something can be done about it by man's own rational efforts.
>
> (p. vii) (my italics)

There can be no doubt that the crucial dangers were evident, and should have been recognised by our intellectuals, not least

151

those working in the Humanities and in education. In his essay 'Human Values in a Changing World', Ludwig von Bertalanffy speaks of a collapse of our whole symbolic system:

> The phenomenon termed nihilism by Nietzsche is nothing else than the imminent breakdown of a symbolic universe . . . The economic symbol of money has lost its connection with reality; a banknote does not represent any more a fixed quantity of gold or of commodities but is subject to continuous re-evaluation, to inflation, sometimes at an astronomical scale and other machinations. Art used to be a symbol-system representative of a certain period in a certain culture. Today's 'art' seems to extend from the finger-painting of a chimpanzee . . . to the homey covers of the *Saturday Evening Post*. Even the symbolic system of science, which is about the only solid thing we have, is shaky in certain aspects and places. The same symbol, democracy, means exactly the opposite when uttered in the West or in the Communist world. The symbolic system of religion which, abstracting from its intrinsic values, at any rate has developed organically in the long course of history, is supplanted by kaleidoscopically changing pseudo-religions, by belief in scientific progress, psychoanalysis, nationalism, soap opera, or tranquillisers.
>
> p. 70

The dignity of man rests on rational behaviour – that is, behaviour directed by symbolic anticipation of a goal. In our time it is being replaced by the 'primitive *vis a tergo* of conditioned reaction'.

Modern methods of propaganda, from toothpaste advertisements to political programmes, do not appeal to rationality, but rather force upon man certain ways of behaviour by continuous repetition of stimuli coupled with emotional rewards or punishments. People are conditioned, not least by appeals to the lowest common denominator, to the lowest intelligence level.

> The result is mass man – that is, abolishment of individual discrimination and decision and its replacement by universal conditioned reflexes.

Another aspect of this problem is cultural regression. Bertalanffy says he is using the term 'regression' in the psychoanalytical sense:

> Partly, even the term 'mental foetalization' in the sense Bolk used the word for certain anatomic characteristics, would seem in place. The

152

comic strip, the peeping tom in the modern form of scandal magazines, the touching infantility of television, the well-filled refrigerator as a sort of nourishing womb, the penis-symbol of the Cadillac, the father image of Eisenhower – all these and many other things are nothing but regression to infantile states ... the attitude is not that of what analysts call the mature ego...

He underlines the nihilistic effect of this regression, which has, of course, grown worse since, not least by the increasing employment of primitive fantasies of sadism and violence.

No wonder, then, that the breakdown of the symbolic universe leads to the experience of being lost in a meaningless world ...

The intellectuals take recourse to existentialist philosophy. He means the 'old' existentialism, which expresses this feeling of loss of meaning, without offering any solution. But for the nonintellectual:

For the many who lack sophistication, there are two other outlets: crime and mental disease. Juvenile delinquency reaching a peak under optimum conditions – what else can it mean but the practice of a philosophy of meaninglessness?

p. 72

In many works of entertainment it is suggested that there is no alternative to endless violence, except a conformity in which one's authenticity was forfeit. Thus our intellectuals have made 'a militant and malicious assault on human values', to quote a leading psychotherapist, Masud R. Khan, speaking of *A Clockwork Orange*.

In wartime in Britain neurotic disorders decreased rather than increased (M. K. Opler, *Culture, Psychiatry and Human Values*, Thomas, 1956, p. 67ff). The suffering of the war did not generate immense mental illness afterwards: recent increases in mental illness have been caused by the collapse of the symbolic superstructure, to which our intellectuals have contributed their endorsement. As Bertalanffy makes plain, culture, as a framework of symbolic values, is not a mere plaything for the human animal or luxury of the intelligentsia; '*it is the very backbone of society, and, among other things, an important psychohygenic factor*'. (my italics, p. 73). The acclaim of cultural nihilism is a contribution to mental illness at large. Bertalanffy is worried in case his argument may prove pessimistic: but he takes hope from the Maslow conference itself, and the way in which these problems were being taken seriously. Alas, in the years since, regression and triviality have deepened, while intellectual resistance has gone over to endorsement of the very ills to which he points. Who could conduct such a symposium now? 'Where there is insight and a will,' he says, 'there might be a way'. But his warning is grave:

> a new symbolic universe of values must be found or an old one reinstated if mankind is to be saved from the pit of meaninglessness, suicide, and atomic fire.

p. 74

Yet, as Masud Khan argues in *The Black Rainbow*, suicide is now almost a condition of consciousness in our civilization, so acute has the feeling of meaninglessness become. Like Camus' *Outsider*, we feel we only feel real because we are condemned to death. Sylvia Plath said much the same thing. We are urged further towards the atomic fire, which must result from the total disintegration of human meaning. How can we avoid our plunge down this abyss? One good source of solutions is to be found by the determined study of philosophical anthropology as recommended in Professor Maslow's symposium, twenty years ago. All Maslow offers us is *work*. For the first time in history, we have the chance of finding something to believe in, through the study of man and his works. Writers like Beckett are trying to involve us in greater apathy, greater paralysis: the Pinters of this world are trying to seduce us into the hatred and fear they have for human existence*. These advocates of nihilism are seeking to prevent us from finding our own potentialities, and to make us blind to possible grounds for something to believe in. We may agree with them that the old symbolic modes have collapsed: but they are telling us

---

* Of course, Beckett is serious in a way Pinter is not, while Pinter is serious in a way pornography and the commercial black cinema are not. But all are nihilistic, and belong to the syndrome of *giving oneself over to the days of hate and non-meaning*. My particular concern is to bring all these things into the compass of a philosophical and educational argument.

('Waiting for Godot') that no symbolic modes are possible. There may be no existing structure of truth and meaning. But at least we now know where to look. There is, as Maslow says, no existing body of value truth. We shall have to create it: all we know is where the work might be done:

> This is not to maintain that this knowledge is *now* available in the final form for breeding conviction and action. It is not. What *is* available, however, is enough to give us confidence that we know the kinds of work that have to be done in order to progress toward such a goal. It appears possible for man, by his own philosophical and scientific efforts, to move towards self-improvement and social improvement.
>
> p. viii

Maslow's Conference on 'New Knowledge in Human Values' was conceived as a first organizing step in this direction. One of the major figures in the movement was Professor Pitrim A. Sorokin, who experienced the mass exterminations and horrors of the First World War, and the Russian revolution. He came to believe that cruelty, hatred and injustice can never create a mental, moral or material millenium, and that the *creative, unselfish work of love for humanity at large* is the key to the reconstruction of the world. So I end my book as I began it, with references to a scientific conference in which some of the leading figures had experienced terrible suffering, but were determined to solve human problems *by love*.

The words 'altruism' and 'love', however, are much less easy on our lips than they were in 1959, since the work of our nihilistic artists and writers. Words have been so corrupted as to make us embarrassed in using them: they, too, have collapsed with the collapse of the symbolic system. Frankl, Meerloo, and Sorokin had actually suffered from the effects of fanatical moral inversion. Yet they forgive, and are devoted to cherishing humanness, in such ways as to make it possible for man, in the future, to try to understand himself, and to avoid such horrors in the future.

Others, like Sylvia Plath, express a hatred of life, and indulge in fantasies of being oppressed. But they have not really been oppressed, and their hatred of human-kind has no such roots. The roots of their hate are in their schizoid condition. And later they become, like Stirner, apathetic. Many sink into

155

an indifferent, aimless, self-destructive egoism, encapsulated, in malignancy or withdrawal, living out their lives, like Sartre, with no further contribution to make to the human world.

Professor Sorokin speaks of 'the unprecedented destructiveness, bestiality, and moral insanity' of the convulsions which he had experienced, and his decision to devote his free time after the war to the study of 'unselfish, creative love, and of effective techniques for transforming the motivational systems of man – and thus transforming his sociocultural universe'. In the meantime, the sociocultural universe itself has been transformed into destructiveness, bestiality and moral insanity by the very intellectuals who should have set their minds against hate. Now Bruno Bettelheim is forced to protest against a film (*Seven Beauties*) which makes a joke of the concentration camps. (*New Yorker*, August 2, 1976).

The scientific symposium which Sorokin organised consisted of a number of distinguished minds, in various disciplines, of whom the contributors to the volume are representative. They included Gordon Allport, Ludwig von Bertalanffy, Jacob Bronowski, Theodosius Dobzhansky, Erich Fromm, Kurt Goldstein, Robert S. Hartman, Gyorgy Kepes, Dorothy Lee, Henry Margenau, Maslow himself and Sorokin: Daisetz Suzuki, a philosopher from Otani University in Japan and an expert on Zen; Paul Tillich, and Walter A. Weisskopf.

This band of distinguished and altruistic thinkers came together in the spirit of Edmund Husserl, whether or not they realized it. The whole idea of philosophy, Husserl felt, must now be revised, and its practical possibilities would be revealed through its execution. 'What should we, who believe, do in order to *be able* to believe?'

Like Husserl, these thinkers were concerned to delineate the limitations of the traditional scientific view: science, he said,

> excludes in principle precisely the questions which man, given over in our times to the most portentous upheavals, finds the most burning questions of the meaning or meaninglessness of human existence. Do not these questions, universal and necessary for all men, demand universal reflections and answers based on rational insight? In the final analysis they concern man as a free self-determining being in his behaviour towards the human and extrahuman surrounding world (*Umwelt*)
> *Crisis.* p 6

156

Husserl speaks out against 'an indifferent turning away', on the part of established philosophy, 'from those questions which are decisive for a genuine humanity' (*Menschentum*). The crisis of science, says Husserl, is the loss of its meaning for life. Humanistic sciences have failed, because their scientific character requires, we are told, that the scholar carefully excludes all valuative positions, all questions of the reason or unreason of their human subject matter and its cultural configurations. Science is concerned with what the world is in fact, and what even the spiritual world is in fact.

> But can the world, and human experience in it, truthfully have a meaning if the sciences recognise as true only what is established in this fashion?
>
> p. 6

How can we console ourselves with that? Can we live in this world, limited to what is to be seen by the science of 'bodies', in which history is nothing but an unending concatenation of illusory progress and bitter disappointment?

The contributors to *New Knowledge in Human Values* set their minds against the world of Newtonian and Galilean science. They recognise that 'in man the biological evolution has transcended itself' (Dobzhansky) and has an added dimension, which is that of the *animal symbolicum*. Moreover, values are rooted in the very conditions of human existence, as biology and the life-sciences are themselves now recognising. Our knowledge of the human condition leads us to establishing values which have objective validity. Some of these values emerge from psychotherapeutic work, such as the ethical relationship between early nurture, psychically speaking, and the capacity of the human being to interact effectively with his world, and to feel that he belongs in a benign world. Maslow declares that humanists have for years been trying to construct a naturalistic, psychological value system, derived from man's nature. Today it is possible for the first time to feel confident that this age-old hope may be fulfilled, if only we work hard enough. He believes, with others in his symposium, that a scientific ethic may be possible, and they believe that they know at least how to go about constructing it.

The essence of this confidence is, as I have suggested above, the discovery of 'centricity': 'organisms,' says Maslow, 'are more self-governing, self-regulating, and autonomous than we thought twenty-five years ago.' He quotes various pieces of work which show that individuals, like some living creatures, left to themselves, make correct choices such as their choice of food. The body has its own wisdom. But, Maslow believes, the human consciousness is capable of making right choices, too.

There are many problems, because there are also bad choosers. Many people simply do not recognise what are the right choices for them, until they are helped to choose by a creative encounter in which they can discover their potentialities to choose. This confirms the psychologies of D. W. Winnicott and Peter Lomas, in which the problem is that of finding the 'true self', which requires collaboration – and variations of love – to enable a person to find his authenticity. But, Maslow believes, there is a fundamental impulse towards self-realization, which is a principle of human existence:

> It looks as if there were a single ultimate value for all mankind, a far goal towards which all men strive. This is called variously by different authors, self-actualization, self-realization, integration, psychological health, individuation, autonomy, creativity, productivity . . . but they all agree that this amounts to realizing the potentialities of the person, that is to say, becoming fully human, everything that a person could become.
>
> p. 12

This conclusion, echoed by other contributors, is a rational, scientific one. Those secondary qualities which Galileo discarded must be made primary, as Hartman insists in this Symposium. Then we may see the truth of that observation which Marion Milner makes, taking a cue from L. L. Whyte, that everyone displays somewhere a 'formative principle', a tendency towards his own 'shape', that which is in him to become.

The vast irrationality which pervades our world is an attempt to fill the vacuum created by scientism, which excludes the whole realm in which these processes go on, as Walter Weisskopf argues. Science has not only excluded important elements of being and existence from its world view, it has de-rationalised the dimension of values. Moreover, insofar

158

as they remained 'objective', the life-sciences seemed to show that values were relative and culture-bound, thus exerting a nihilistic influence on values themselves, since these came to seem unreal. In the combination of these scientific denials of his essential existence with the economic reduction of his life to the functional and economic planes, modern man cannot but feel that everything that makes life worth living is unreal, and so he suffers from existential frustration.

The scientific point of view to which the contributors to Maslow's symposium are groping is one which recognises as a fact that 'the ultimate ground of values is rooted in the ultimate ground of being.' (p. 109)

> Whereas the biology of the nineteenth century emphasized the role of the struggle for existence, the biology of our time more and more emphasizes – whether in evolution of species or in survival of separate species, or in maintenance of health, vitality and longevity – the factor of mutual aid, cooperation and friendship, all these terms being but different words designating diverse aspects of the same creative unselfish love.
>
> Sorokin, p. 5

As Sorokin argues, communities founded on love last long, while those based on hate have a very short life. And there are growing discoveries of the reality and effectiveness of love's mysterious force in natural processes.

Maslow brings together many kinds of investigation, to suggest that there are certain fundamental needs recognised in the area of love and meaning. People have the capacity to love, and need to love in order to be healthy. The need for meaning is a major psychological need. Such psychic needs must be recognised as much as the need for salt, or vitamins. The individual yearns for the gratification of these needs. Their deprivation makes the person sicken and wither, or stunts his growth. Gratifying people's inner needs is therapeutic, curing the deficiency illness, while steady supplies forestall these illnesses, and healthy people do not demonstrate them (p. 123).

> The human being has within him a pressure (among other pressures) toward unity of personality, towards spontaneous expressiveness, toward full individuality and identity, *toward seeing the truth rather than being blind,*

toward being good, and a lot else ... pressing toward serenity, kindness, courage, knowledge, honesty, love, unselfishness, and goodness.

p. 126 (my italics)

Such a statement strikes us today as unbelievable, breathless audacity. The whole tide of our culture has become devoted to denying and negating all these human capacities, and exposing them to a cynical nihilism, and hate.

Maslow specifically rejects the Freudian, natural science, view of man's relationship to civilisation:

> We can now reject, as a localism, the almost universal mistake that the interests of the individual and of society are necessarily mutually exclusive and antagonistic, or that civilization is primarily a mechanism for controlling and policing human instinctoid impulses. All these age-old axioms are swept away by the new possibility of defining the main function of a healthy culture and each of its institutions as the fostering of universal self-actualization.

p. 129

Maslow, whose work is based on the study of healthy human beings, asks what is the reward for the 'becoming' of the individual. People wish for a 'something'. These inclinations cannot be satisfied without the discovery of causes to which the individual devotes himself: as Viktor Frankl argues, 'demand quality' is an important factor. But Maslow finds the reward of becoming in *Being*. From time to time, every individual, if he is healthy, feels a 'peak experience': a housewife cooking a meal, a man digging and planting his garden, or an author finishing a book. It comes to everyone who, in any way, achieves a sense of self-transcendence, by some act of care, or love, or creativity, or of insight and understanding. These are our glimpses of 'Heaven', and it is these feelings of transcendence and realization that make life worth living. We remember them during the difficult or painful episodes of life.

> We are again and again rewarded for good becoming by transient states of absolute being, which I have summarised as peak experiences ... Achieving basic-need gratifications give us many peak-experiences, each of which are absolute delights, perfect in themselves, and needing no more than themselves to validate life.

p. 124

Besides these outstanding feelings of achievement, there are continual 'foothill experiences', 'little moments of being'. Being and Becoming are not contradictory, or mutually exclusive. Approaching and arriving are both in themselves rewarding.

Samuel Beckett's world is one in which no such becoming, or being, is possible: and this is so *in nearly all modern art*. In obscene drama, in 'expendable' art, in 'Beat' poetry*, the transcendent moment of meaning, peak moments, are denied us: even the *attempt* to create meaning is discredited, by the reduction of art to the chance, to the disposable, to the schizophrenic substitution of the concrete for the symbolic and creative.

In George Kepes' comments in this symposium, love and art are linked. Art belongs to formative processes of inter-subjectivity. Science brings a sense of order and meaning, by its descriptions of the world. Art provides the 'joy of felt order' – inner order. But today, 'the artist has timidly reduced his vistas to the narrow ranges of reacting to personal hurts.' In other words schizoid influences were already beginning to wreck the symbolic complex, by dragging art down to the expression of crippled souls, whose degrading view of man excludes all those capacities for 'peak moments' which Donne, Shakespeare, Keats, and Chaucer convey to us. This collapse in art is not a question of condition or circumstance: Isaac Rosenberg wrote a 'peak-moment' poem facing death in the trenches, while D. H. Lawrence wrote *Roses on the Breakfast Table*, in the same sequence as *Song of a Man who is Not Loved*. It is rather that the arts have failed and plunged into the chasm, at the very moment when a rational approach to human nature has found what Maslow calls 'the unseen planet with *had* to be there' – meaning. Even as it becomes possible, for the first time, to set the grounds of human meaning-in-Being against the ghastly prophesies of Nietzsche, our intellectuals and culture-followers, journalists, and *even those working in the Humanities in education*, those who should uphold values in a barbarous world, have turned treacherous. And worse than

*I am thinking of Ernst Jandl's contribution to *Wholly Communion*, Lorrimer, 1965: and Trocchi's. See also my *Lost Bearings in English Poetry*.

that. Not content with betrayal, they have created, hardened, and defended a position of false solutions, moral inversion and chaos, from which it is almost impossible to recover. Once the symbolic system has been allowed to be broken down and corrupted, the very apparatus by which we may avoid the atomic fire ceases to be available. It is like a plant, which might recover by care from a little wilting: but once it has dried out, or has lost too much foliage, or has forfeited too much of its substance by drooping and withering, a point is reached from which no recovery is possible. Only by the most strenuous and urgent methods can we now find sufficient meaning to survive.

In Maslow's time, it was possible to feel that we might avoid catastrophe. We could envisage a new future for man, by hard work, in the area of the search for true humanist values. Today, the first problem is to restore enough morale to believe it is worth trying to believe.

SELECTED BIBLIOGRAPHY

Abbs, Peter, (Ed), *The Black Rainbow*, Heinemann, 1976

Allchin, W. H., *Young People: Problems of Adaptation*, Guild of Pastoral Psychology, 1970

Bantock, G. H., *Culture, Industrialization and Edcation*, Routledge, 1968

Bellow, Saul, *Mr Sammler's Planet*, Penguin Books, 1970

Beveridge, Ian, *The Art of Scientific Investigation*, Heinemann, 1950

Binswanger, Ludwig, *Being in the World*, Souvenir Press, 1975

Buytendijk, F. J. J. passages in *Approaches to a Philosophical Biology*, Grene, q.v.

Cassirer, Ernst, *An Essay on Man*, Yale, 1944

Cooke, Deryck, *The Language of Music*, Oxford, 1959

Drury, M. O'C., *The Danger of Words*, Routledge, 1973

Erikson, Erik H., *Childhood And Society*, Penguin Books, 1950

Fairbairn, W. R. D., *Psychoanalytic Studies of the Personality*, Tavistock, 1952

Farber, Leslie H., *The Ways of the Will*, Constable, 1966

Frankl, Viktor, *From Death Camp to Existentialism*, later *The Search for Meaning*, Beacon Press, 1962

– *The Doctor and the Soul*, Souvenir, 1969

– *Psychotherapy and Existentialism*, Souvenir, 1970

– see Koestler, A. *The Alpbach Seminar.*

Friedman, Maurice, and Schilpp P. A. (Eds) *The Philosophy of Martin Buber*, Cambridge, 1967

Grene, Marjorie, *Dreadful Freedom*, later *An Introduction to Existentialism*, Chicago, 1948

– *The Knower and the Known*, Faber, 1966

– *Approaches to a Philosophical Biology*, Basic Books, 1968
Guntrip, Harry, *Personality Structure and Human Interaction*, Hogarth, 1961
– *Schizoid Phenomena, Object Relations and the Self*, Hogarth, 1968
Henry, Jules, *Culture Against Man*, Tavistock, 1966
Holbrook, David, (Ed) *The Case Against Pornography*, Stacey, 1972. (Especially the contributions by Mary Miles, Masud Khan, and David Boadella).
Hudson, Liam, *The Cult of the Fact*, Cape, 1972
Husserl, Edmund, *The Crisis of European Sciences*, Northwestern, 1970
Jung, C. G., *Man and His Symbols*, Aldus, 1964
Koestler, Arthur, and Smithies, Robert, *The Alpbach Seminar*, Hutchinson, 1969. (Especially the contribution by Viktor Frankl)
Laing, R. D., *The Divided Self*, Tavistock, 1960
– *The Politics of Experience*, Penguin Books, 1967
Langer, Susanne, *Philosophy in a New Key*, Harvard, 1963
– *Philosophical Sketches*, Hopkins, 1962
Lawrence, D. H., *The Rainbow*, Heinemann, 1915
Leavis, F. R., *The Living Principle*, Chatto, 1976
Ledermann, E. K., *Existential Neurosis*, Butterworth, 1972
Macbeth, Norman, *Darwin Retried*, Garnstone, 1971
MacMurray, John, *Religion, Art and Science*, Liverpool, 1961
Marcel, Gabriel, *The Philosophy of Existence*, Harvill, 1948
Maslow, Abraham, *Towards a Psychology of Being*, Von Nostrand, 1968
– (Ed) *New Knowledge in Human Values*, Von Nostrand, 1959
May, Rollo, *Love and Will*, Souvenir Press, 1969
– *Power and Innocence*, Souvenir Press, 1972
– (Ed) *Existence – a New Dimension in Psychiatry*, Basic Books, 1958
Milner, Marion, *On Not Being Able to Paint*, Heinemann, 1950
– *In the Hands of the Living God*, Hogarth, 1969
Murdoch, Iris, *Sartre*, Bowes and Bowes, 1953
Paterson, R. W. K., *The Nihilistic Egoist, Max Stirner*, Hull, 1971
Plessner, Helmuth, *Laughing and Crying*, Northwestern, 1970
Polanyi, Michael, *Science, Faith and Society*, Chicago, 1946

– *Knowing and Being*, Routledge, 1969
– *Personal Knowledge*, Routledge, 1958
– (with Harry Prosch) *Meaning*, Chicago, 1975
Poole, Roger, *Towards Deep Subjectivity*, Allen Lane, 1972
– *Empiricism in Crisis, Tract 21*, Gryphon Press, 1977
Roubiczek, Paul, *Existentialism, For and Against*, Cambridge, 1964
Rieff, Phillip, *Fellow Teachers*, Faber, 1975
Robinson, Ian, *The Survival of English*, Cambridge, 1975
Roszak, Theodore, *Where the Wasteland Ends*, Faber, 1972
Stoller, Robert, *Perversion: the Erotic Form of Hatred*, Harvester Press, 1976
Towers, Bernard, *Concerning Teilhard*, Collins, 1969
– with John Lewis, *Naked Ape – or Homo Sapiens?* Garnstone, 1969
Winnicott, D. W., *Playing and Reality*, Tavistock, 1971
– *The Family and Individual Development*, Tavistock, 1965
– *Therapeutic Consultations in Child Psychiatry*, Hogarth, 1971

INDEX

167

168